JOY WORKS

Empowering Teams in the New Era of Work

ALEX LIU

Managing Partner and
Chairman of the Board, Kearney

WILEY

Published by John Wiley & Sons, Inc., Hoboken, New Jersey.
Published simultaneously in Canada.

For general information on our other products and services or for technical support, please contact our Customer Care Department within the United States at (800) 762-2974, outside the United States at (317) 572-3993 or fax (317) 572-4002.

Wiley also publishes its books in a variety of electronic formats. Some content that appears in print may not be available in electronic formats. For more information about Wiley products, visit our web site at www.wiley.com.

Library of Congress Cataloging-in-Publication Data

Names: Liu, Alex (Management consultant), author.
Title: Joy works : empowering teams in the new era of work / Alex Liu.
Description: Hoboken, New Jersey : John Wiley & Sons, Inc., [2023] |
   Includes index.
Identifiers: LCCN 2022032951 (print) | LCCN 2022032952 (ebook) | ISBN
   9781119988052 (hardback) | ISBN 9781119988076 (adobe pdf) | ISBN
   9781119988069 (epub)
Subjects: LCSH: Work—Social aspects. | Work—Psychological aspects. |
   Quality of work life. | Joy.
Classification: LCC HD6955 .L574 2023 (print) | LCC HD6955 (ebook) | DDC
   306.3/6—dc23/eng/20220907
LC record available at https://lccn.loc.gov/2022032951
LC ebook record available at https://lccn.loc.gov/2022032952

Cover Design: Wiley
Cover Image and Author Photo: © A.T. Kearney, Inc.

SKY10036127_092222

This book is dedicated to the next generation. May we all work to build a future of work that brings joy, purpose, and energy for you. It's always a relay race to the future.

Contents

Acknowledgments

Thank you to ...

- All of the joyful leaders who shared your time, reflections, and insights for this book. I am continuously inspired by each one of you.
- My Kearney team of teams around the world for their daily pursuit of excellence in building clients, capabilities, and our culture.
- My dedicated provocateurs and co-conspirators on this timely topic, Abby Klanecky, Kristin Boswell, Lee Price, and Marty McPadden.
- My beloved mother and father, Lilyon and Shia-ling, who respectively showed me the virtues of being relentless and joyful at the same time, filling myself with both hope and gratitude always.
- My many coaches, teachers, mentors, and family who showed belief in me throughout the years, and from whom I learned to passionately and confidently do what I love and love what I do.

Foreword

By Charlene Thomas, Executive Vice President and Chief Diversity, Equity and Inclusion Officer, UPS.

Joy. It's as specific as a fingerprint, as common as a garden rose. At times, for some, it's as elusive as a four-leaf clover.

But we keep reaching toward joy. It's the pinnacle. The manifestation of happiness. The reward at the end of the rainbow.

And joy at work? To me, joy at work should be an everyday lived experience. Something we sow throughout our careers, not a reward that is delivered through paychecks, promotions, or the final reward of retirement.

For leaders at every level, the defining question each day should be: **How do we create the conditions for joy to exist, for ourselves and those around us?**

Let's back up for a minute. I'm Charlene Thomas. I'm a leader, a Peloton superfan, a scuba diver, a mother, a college football enthusiast (Roll Tide!), and a 33-year (and counting) employee of UPS. My tenure at UPS has taken me around the United States, from a part-time job in college to driving a UPS truck outside Philadelphia to leading operations and package delivery teams in Maryland, Alabama, Arizona, and California. Now I'm a corporate leader at our headquarters in Atlanta, focused on diversity and inclusion for our 500,000-plus employees worldwide.

I have moved around a lot, and done a lot of different jobs, but most of my career experiences have followed a fairly standard formula:

- ◆ Connect with your new team immediately. Meet them in their environment. Get to know the people—their strengths, weaknesses, and relationships with each other. Get to know something about them personally as well as professionally.
- ◆ Listen for understanding. Separate the noise from true substance.
- ◆ Empower the team to solve the problems they have the resources to handle.
- ◆ Remove the barriers.
- ◆ Define success, celebrate wins often, and include learnings from previous losses.

I have repeated that equation over and over with teams of all sizes. My experiences have taught me about people, about motivation, and about management. But above all, I have learned about joy.

Here's what I have learned:

Achieving joy is not about you. It's not about individual success. It's about a shared outcome. On a team, everyone's contribution is necessary, and it's always a team effort. Winning is achieving the outcome for everyone equally.

Joy never requires someone else to lose. We don't all win unless everyone wins. If there are losers, you aren't winning. Joy requires collective equity. Your joy won't be fully realized if it requires someone else to sacrifice or compromise. We can't rely on subjugating or compromising someone else in order to make it out on top.

Joy requires intention. Joy at work doesn't just happen spontaneously. It requires nurturing, engagement, and intention. At any given moment, if people don't understand what their purpose is, their work won't bring them joy. But when we're intentional about communicating the purpose and create a path for everyone to achieve their aspiration equitably, we can find true joy.

Joy and fun go hand in hand. We can't forget to have fun! In corporate cultures, we can get very serious and focused on tasks. But joy is about celebrating achievements, amplifying small moments, and leaning into euphoria. Never miss an opportunity to celebrate and amplify a positive outcome.

Joy is the fuel that keeps us going. That's why I'm thrilled that Alex Liu is addressing this topic in this book. I'm proud to be a part of the movement for more collective joy at work.

When the world feels scary and the challenges ahead are hard, we have to choose joy. Intentional, collective joy is the answer. Joy is our path forward. When we choose joy, we make progress together.

Introduction

Why joy matters to me

Pick a phrase to describe myself? It would likely be "joyfully relentless." But joy is the juice. That's why joy is a topic I've been actively exploring for the past five years—and implicitly for decades before that.

Why joy? Why joy at work? Why now?

The short answer is: **Why would we settle for anything else?**

When there is a clear lack of something in the world, it's human nature to seek it, anywhere. In the recent past, there has been no shortage of mayhem, uncertainty, and despair of semi-biblical proportions. Is the pursuit of joy a kneejerk reaction to the day and age, or is it more fundamental? We are born happy, in our parents' arms. As children, we're brimming with joy. Even when we face big firsts—first day of school, first day on a new job—we're optimistic and can find joy in the unknown opportunities ahead of us.

What happens as adults that makes us despair and disengage?

I likely inherited my calm sense of optimism from my dad, whose life certainly was not easy. Growing up as a poor peasant in rural China, he had 10 siblings and was the only kid in the family to get past an eighth-grade education. My parents came to the United States as immigrants from Taiwan when I was a baby, and my father built his career as a professor, teaching at historically Black colleges and universities in the US South. Because he was not white, he wasn't allowed to teach white kids. Having endured wars, revolution, racism, and hostility in various doses throughout his life, he always kept his cool in a way that steeled all those around him, including me.

My life certainly has been much easier than his, but it wasn't always sunshine and roses. I was the only Asian kid in my North Carolina town in the 1960s. I looked for ways to build belonging, mostly through sports. Early in my life, I learned the power of teams to build rapport and learn the unwritten rules about acceptance. If people looked at me funny when I walked onto the Little League field, all I had to do was start fielding and hitting, and then I became just one of the team.

My dad taught me this: Regardless of the things you go through, you'll find peace if you're happy with where you are, grateful for what you have, and find a way to belong.

Those childhood lessons have stayed with me throughout my career.

The most renewable energy resource is human energy. Finding a way to uncork your energy is important, especially in tough times. Life isn't a linear progression, where every day is better than the one before. We go a few steps forward, then a few back.

That means life is more like a vector. A vector is a mathematical term for an object that has both force and direction. It's an arrow. Your direction might be toward fulfillment, happiness, connection, and belonging. But that's not enough. You need the force of day-to-day energy and purpose: What's my sense of meaning when my feet hit the floor every morning? Even when times are tough, I need to have something to look forward to. And it's up to me to adapt and keep my energy, my force, and my direction moving.

For me, joy is my momentum and my life force. Joy gives me that energy. I re-create that energy and come back to it every day. I want the people I influence to capture the same moment. I don't want to settle for anything less. None of us should.

Joy at work

Joy isn't just a personal pursuit. I quickly learned the importance of joy at work, too.

After college and business school, I stumbled into consulting. I loved it because I was constantly encountering new ideas. Consulting is the hidden growth industry. It's an index for change in our broader social and economic universe. When companies are facing major change and transformation, they often call on consultants to help them make sense of it, and to adapt.

Coming from a family of teachers and coaches, I loved an industry that's all about helping companies, teams, and individuals achieve their full potential. I embraced the team environment, just like on a Little League team: Are we gonna win the championship this year?

In my early days, people called me the "mood manager." I was the class provocateur and jokester, throwing my rugby ball around in the conference room, making friends, and enjoying my time on teams. I knew that I had to stay open and curious to be good at my job and to enjoy it. My models and mentors showed me how to stay open to learning and to my natural curiosity.

A few years ago, I took on the role of managing partner and chairman at Kearney. Leading a global team of teams—a global people business with thousands of colleagues—provided me a perfect platform for **joy** as an inspirational touchstone and guiding principle. Consulting is a people business, but I don't want the people at the firm to "perform." I want them to *thrive*.

As a start, we did some research to understand the current state of joy at work for people around the world. We asked people what they expect from work versus what they actually feel. We quickly identified a troubling **joy gap:** More than half of the working adults we surveyed feel less joy at work than they'd expect—across all generations, geographies, and organizational levels. That original survey was in 2018, and when we surveyed again three years later, the joy gap had grown even more. The joy gap is real and has been for a while.

It affects people in all kinds of companies: small businesses and big companies, start-ups and established firms, in all industries. And it affects people at all levels in an organization, from entry level to the C-suite.

Most people want work that is fulfilling, positive, and inspiring. So why do so few of us actually have that experience?

I have a few ideas.

People, praise, and purpose

Our firm has doubled down on understanding joy at work, and our research has found three major difference-makers: people, praise, and purpose.

First, **people**. The pandemic banished us all to our distant corners, and through that isolation, we learned the value of community and social connections. We missed our neighbors, our colleagues, and our friends.

Finding a way to foster social connection at work is a primary way to keep the forward force of joy in your organization.

Second, **praise**. We all want to be acknowledged for our efforts, contributions, and successes. Leaders who are generous and specific with their praise build more joyful teams.

Finally, the big one: **purpose**. We'll talk a lot more about purpose in this book because it's such an important baseline condition for joy. When we understand our organization's purpose and our very specific role in that broader purpose, we can unlock new motivation, satisfaction, and joy. I am inspired by the Japanese word *ikigai*, which roughly translates as "a reason for being." We'll explore *ikigai* more in Chapter 5.

Joy, justice, and a better world

That's the baseline for why joy matters to me—personally and at work.

But where does joy fit in a world that is navigating complicated, painful divisions and reckonings?

In 2019, I started hosting a podcast called Joy@Work. In those pre-pandemic days (remember those?), I wanted to explore how to build more joy at work. In my conversations with podcast guests, I asked questions about how to design a happier office space, how to capture passion and creativity, and how to build community at work.

Then the pandemic hit. As the world spiraled and the inequity and pain hidden just below the surface started to bubble up, "joy" took on a much deeper meaning.

I still interviewed guests on the podcast, but suddenly, we weren't talking about happy paint colors or how to plan office team-building events.

Joy led to justice, to mission and purpose, to building work in a way that is sustainable for the human spirit and sustainable for our planet.

We explored what I call the ABCs: allyship, belonging, and culture.

As my Kearney teams hunkered down in their homes around the world, I started writing a weekly email to my colleagues. I focused on the ABCs and asked for insight: How could we build more belonging at Kearney and do the same for our clients?

In the summer of 2020, I wrote:

Let's continue to be great allies to each other in all ways,
as we strive for and achieve greater belonging for all of us.
We deserve that aspirational culture.

Like many leaders around the world, I worked on reflecting and listening. And I heard that people wanted to feel **seen, supported, and inspired.** They needed to feel cared for and respected. I take that challenge seriously, and it has become my driving force.

The future of joy at work

So how can we think about building a future of work that is joyful? To answer that question, I look to the generations that are coming up behind me.

As I write this, I am almost five years into my role as managing partner at Kearney. At this point, I think I'm one of the oldest people at the firm. Seventy-nine percent of our colleagues are Millennials or Gen Z. Most of the work at the firm is done by these future generations.

Leading the next generations has made me humble. I hear a few standout themes loud and clear from my Gen Y and Gen Z colleagues at Kearney:

We need a broader definition of corporate success. Revenue and profits aren't the be-all, end-all. Ditto for shareholder value. Instead, there's a push for sustainability, stakeholder capitalism, multilateralism, and inclusivity. Employees are not going to settle for being a cog in a company, churning out corporate profits.

Work should make people feel psychologically and physically safe, supported, and inspired. The pandemic drove home the need to keep people physically safe, but there's an equally important psychological and emotional element: treating people with respect, seeing them for who they are, and supporting them as they grow and evolve.

The future of work is about purpose and meaning. Increasingly, people demand work cultures that are rooted in purpose. And leaders around the world are paying attention. As Unilever CEO Alan Jope said in 2020, "Brands with purpose grow, companies with purpose last, and people with purpose thrive."

In this book, I'll use these noble and inspiring goals to guide our exploration into joy at work.

As I said, leading the next generations has been humbling for me. I'm determined to continue my lifelong focus on joy, friendship, teamwork, curiosity, and learning. Instead of shutting down the next generations' push toward change, I'm responding: "Tell me more. Help me build it."

And: **"Why would we settle for anything less?"**

Who you'll hear from in this book

This book started with my perspective as a leader, backed by my firm's research about joy at work. But as you'll see in the pages that follow, I called on many other people to share their stories, perspectives, and ideas about shifting to joy. I'm grateful to my friends, old and new, who reflected with me and agreed to let me print excerpts of our conversations here.

In this book, you'll hear from the following people:

- Crystal Ashby, former CEO of the Executive Leadership Council (ELC)
- Dr. Dan Cable, professor of organizational behavior at London Business School
- Ken Davenport, Tony Award–winning Broadway producer
- Gerri Elliott, former chief sales and marketing officer at Cisco
- Callie Field, president of T-Mobile's business group
- Hubert Joly, former CEO of Best Buy and author of *The Heart of Business*
- Laura Lane, chief corporate affairs officer at UPS
- Ingrid Fetell Lee, designer and author of *Joyful*
- Jon Levy, behavioral scientist and author of *You're Invited*
- Kathryn Minshew, co-founder of The Muse and author of *The New Rules of Work*
- Michael J. Nyenhuis, president and CEO of UNICEF USA
- Kathryn Parsons, founder of Decoded
- Andrew Suniula, USA Rugby coach
- Stephen Tang, former CEO of OraSure
- Alicia Tillman, former CMO of SAP
- Brian Tippens, former chief sustainability officer at HPE
- Dr. Ashley Whillans, professor at Harvard Business School
- Dr. Anthony Wilbon, dean of the Howard School of Business

Who this book is for

If you're interested in creating more joy—in your own life, on your work team, and in your broader organization—this book is for you.

I wrote this book for a variety of people:

- **The leaders** who hear the demand for more joy, meaning, and purpose, but aren't sure how to shift their corporate cultures
- **The managers** who are facing pressures from above (better margins, higher productivity, more results) and pressures from below (more work–life balance, more joy, more meaning)
- **The young people** who are adamant that they can have a life and a career that's centered on joy and meaning
- **And anyone** who thinks "joy at work" is a near-term possibility, not an impossible oxymoron

Let's build more joy.

Throughout the book, you'll find specific ideas you can try on your own team. Look for the

---

→ **TRY THIS:** callouts for quick experiments to shift toward joy at work.

CHAPTER 1

Why Business Leaders Should Prioritize Joy at Work

In this book, you'll read arguments for joy at work and the profound impact that joy can have on an organization. We'll cover the importance of joy for people, for an organization's broader purpose, and for making progress on major societal issues that extend beyond a company's walls. But before we dive in any further, I want to make the business case for joy at work.

Joy is your biggest business opportunity

You might be thinking, "I run a business. What does joy have to do with my work? Isn't this just a nice-to-have? Is joy really a serious business concern? And are leaders really responsible for employees' emotions?"

Here's my answer to that question. Don't push joy aside as a side issue. If you look deeper, you'll realize that joy is a baseline for a lot of the key elements you need to lead a successful organization. Joy is about positive teamwork. It's about stimulating belief and confidence in the collective goal and business mission. Winning impact. Successful recruiting and retention. It's about people. Isn't this what business and personal execution are all about?

Shouldn't you have a point of view on the human energy that powers your organization?

Leaders who don't understand their people or culture won't easily understand that joy is, in fact, the highest aspiration. Because creating a culture of joy at work means that people willingly give their energy to the company. They form powerful teams that make things happen, help each other, and look for new ways to solve your most pressing problems.

And even if you're not responsible for how other people feel, per se, I would argue that leaders *are* responsible for creating a work environment that supports joy. Because who wants to build a workplace that keeps people from feeling joy?

Creating joy? It's a prerequisite for a high-performing team. It's not an idea to leave to HR to think about. It's your biggest business opportunity.

JOY = PURPOSE ACTIVATED

If you're getting stuck on the idea of "joy," maybe "purpose" will feel more natural to you.

At Kearney, we think about purpose as a timeless, core force that allows individuals and organizations to live their reason for being.

Joy and purpose are closely related. You could argue that joy is purpose activated. When we activate and act on our purpose (as individuals, teams, and organizations), we experience joy. All of these big themes are interrelated: purpose, vision, mission, culture, and joy. I think of joy as the glue that holds it all together.

Purpose is a powerful lever for change. And the research backs that up. More purposeful organizations—organizations where people feel joy in moments of acting on their purpose—outperform on all dimensions.

Purpose-activated companies have:

- **Better employee performance and retention.** Employees are 4 times more likely to give extra, and 11 times more committed to staying.[1]
- **Faster growth.** Certified B-Corps (companies with a defined social and environmental impact) show dramatically higher growth rates, especially in consumer-driven industries.[2] Additionally, Babson Professor Raj Sisojdia studied "conscious," purpose-driven enterprises over a 15-year period. The conscious companies outperformed the S&P 500 index by a factor of 10.5.[3]

Joy powers execution

At Kearney, our teams often help design, co-create, and guide transformations alongside our clients. And over several decades doing this work, I have learned that when a transformation is failing, it's generally *not* because the strategy from the top is wrong. It's because the execution from the middle is lacking. That's where the real power is: who can say no, versus who says yes.

---

[1] Great Place to Work Report 2017: https://info.greatplacetowork.no/hubfs/ Premiuminnhold/Rapporter/3%20Predictions%20for%20the%20Workplace %20Culture%20of%20the%20Future100_Best_Report_2017_2.5b.pdf

[2] "B Corp Analysis Reveals Purpose-Led Businesses Grow 28 Times Faster Than National Average." Sustainable Brands, https://sustainablebrands.com/read/ business-case/b-corp-analysis-reveals-purpose-led-businesses-grow-28-times-faster-than-national-average#:~:text=New%20research%20from%20B%20 Corp,economic%20growth%20of%200.5%20percent

[3] Tony Schwartz, "Companies That Practice "Conscious Capitalism" Perform 10x Better," *Harvard Business Review*, April 4, 2013, https://hbr.org/2013/04/ companies-that-practice-conscious-capitalism-perform

So why does execution fall apart? Why do organizations fail to deliver on their goals? Simple: It's all about people. Execution falls apart because people aren't linked together and tuned in.

Or, especially in recent times, maybe it's just too hard. People wonder: Why are leaders now asking me to work across boundaries and siloes with people I don't even know, to become more digitally fluent, to develop my understanding of diversity and inclusion, all while working from home, taking care of home matters, while reading of horrific news on a real-time basis? If the job is simply transactional to them—just getting through the day—then the execution will flounder. It's just not worth it.

We hear a lot about "change management." At its core, change management is about motivating and enabling people to do things differently, to align their sense of meaning with the company's need to always get better. If we need people to get from A to B, we need them to buy into the change, understand the strategy, understand how their personal purpose aligns with the broader institutional purpose, and use their own internal motivation to do their part to create change and do things differently.

Our own work on business transformation shows that the most successful change programs embed employee engagement and other informal motivators. We have found that those programs are more likely to succeed than programs that fail to include the same joy triggers (we'll talk more about these joy triggers in Chapter 2).

When we lead with one eye on joy, when we can connect at a more fundamental human level, we can tap into the power of people—an organization's renewable energy source. We can move forward, together, in a shared direction.

Joy is critical for all kinds of business

Let's say you work in a service business. Your organization's success relies on happy customers. They want to feel heard. They want their needs met. Which means you need happy employees to develop those positive relationships. Employees who are tuned in and in tune will sense what customers need and provide what customers want. They will come to work ready to make people feel welcome. But if employees are just punching the clock and praying for their next break, or scanning job listings for a better gig elsewhere? Forget it. Your customers will look elsewhere, too. The market research validates this, but it's intuitive too. How many of you remember how you felt at the dinner table when your mother or father came home from work, happy or less so? Didn't their mood affect yours? It's the same at work, and with your customers.

If you're in a product business, you'll also need joyful people on your team. Joyful employees are always trying to make the product better. Joyful employees look for new ways to innovate on the product and listen closely for new ideas. If they work in a store where your customers buy the product, they care about stocking the shelves properly, answering questions, and creating a positive environment. Without joy, all of that dedication, focus, and innovation is—poof—gone.

Joy is the foundation for many key business metrics

Do you see what I'm getting at? Joy is not just "soft stuff." It's the juice that drives people to do the best version of their job, and even inspires them to broaden their job role.

If a company's leadership is setting a direction, joy is what powers the movement in that direction. Joy is the force and the energy. Joy is a proxy for the belief, conviction, confidence, forward momentum, and team dedication that you need to execute on any strategy.

Saying you don't care about joy is like saying you don't care about the team, the product, the customer, the marketplace, or the future of your organization. Joy creates the conditions for a lasting, sustainable business. If you're a CEO who isn't particularly interested in the people at your organization, I'd bet you won't be CEO for long. Our experience working on change inside organizations has shown us that "followership" happens when leaders model the desired behaviors and are authentic in their commitment to their people, being honest but objective, telling their own stories on their "why," as much as the collective why.

I see a new wave of successful executives who are tapping into a new dimension of leadership that wasn't highly valued 20 or 30 years ago. We're seeing a new recipe: leaders who are more authentic and vulnerable. Leaders who have high emotional intelligence (EQ), not just high IQ. Leaders from multiple disciplines—not just engineering, but human sociology. People who are more diverse, with broader backgrounds than we saw represented in boardrooms of the past. We've seen this happen before. For a while, business culture favored CEOs with sales backgrounds; then there was a wave of leaders with finance backgrounds, or consulting, or technology, or startups. But now, we're in an era that calls for leaders with expertise in the human arts. Or maybe we always have been yearning for this kind of leader, but we weren't explicitly looking!

Leaders can't defer "the soft stuff" or "the people stuff" to their HR department. There's no way around it: If there's a people problem, it is your problem. You own that opportunity. The people requirement is so important that every leader needs to step up and set the tone and the agenda for all people topics. It's the only way to get the maximum energy and impact from everyone at the company.

Middle managers and . . . joy?

Let's get back to "moving the middle" of an organization. When I think about examples of joy, I think about the very top (inspiring leaders who set a bold new vision and empower the people around them to make big decisions) and the bottom (the front-line employees who deliver powerful experiences for customers and leave an impression). But what about all of the people in the middle of an organization? Can we inspire individuals, while also empowering teams with purpose?

If you're going on a change journey, you need to bring along the people in the middle of the company. Why the middle? Because that's where the real power lives in a company. The middle managers are the ones who can say no—and often do. It's most easily seen in passive-aggressive behavior, not outward resistance: Initiatives don't get funding or resources, timelines magically extend, and the messengers (and sometimes even the consultants) get blamed. Momentum stalls.

It makes sense. Why would middle managers say "yes" to big change and disruption? Why would they rock the boat, put their position at risk, or make their work harder? They've worked their way to a comfortable place. It's much easier and safer to stay the course and stick with the status quo than to power big, radical changes or question what's working. Easier to keep doing things the way they've always been done. Dig in with a smile, and this too shall pass.

Middle managers may resist change because they understand the massive amount of work the change will require—and they lack the capacity in their day-to-day jobs and lives to take on more.

That's where joy comes in. What if we infused the middle of our companies with joy? What if we brought in the energy from the youngest generations? What if we imbued the work with a new sense of optimism? What if we empowered middle managers to say "yes" just as often as they said "no"? To take risks, to think beyond their box? What if we incentivized people to embrace big change, instead of buckling up and riding it out?

Joy can create capacity—and not just in terms of people wanting to work harder and longer. When we have a lens of joy, we're empowered to stop doing lower-value work and make more room in our day for new ideas. In fact, I believe that most people, including middle managers, *want* to change but struggle to find the time they need to innovate and rethink their work.

What if we rethink the stereotypes about the middle, and instead create middle management that is inspired, full of momentum, purpose, and joy? I think that rethinking the middle could lead to a tidal wave of joy at organizations all over the world.

Finally, I'll say this: We all have blind spots. You, me, everyone else. But if you find yourself still thinking, "Joy isn't important," I have news for you. That's your blind spot. And it's in your best interest to rethink that position and open your mind to the growing importance of joy in your organization, right now and in the future.

If you want to be a top-performing leader, or run a top-performing organization, put joy on the agenda.

Give yourself permission to feel the feeling of joy.
We hold ourselves back from joy because we associate it with being juvenile or silly. We worry that if we express joy too visibly—if we laugh too loud or are too playful— we will be dismissed as not serious or superficial or frivolous. When you feel that urge to hold yourself back from joy, take a moment to let go of that.

—Ingrid Fetell Lee, designer and
author of *Joyful*

CHAPTER 2

What the Research Tells Us About Joy

First, let's dig deeper into our research about joy at work. As I shared in the introduction, my firm, Kearney, has been studying the "joy gap"—the troubling discrepancy between how many people *expect* to feel joy from their work and how many people *actually* experience joy.

The joy gap is real

In 2018, we surveyed people around the world and asked: How much joy do you *expect* to experience at work? And how much joy do you *actually* experience?[1] Nearly 90 percent of respondents said they expect to experience a substantial degree of joy at work. But only 37 percent report that they *actually* experience substantial joy at work. That leaves 53 percent of people who are coming up short on joy. They feel less joy than they'd hope.

---

[1]https://www.kearney.com/leadership-change-organization/article/-/insights/joy-in-the-new-era-of-work

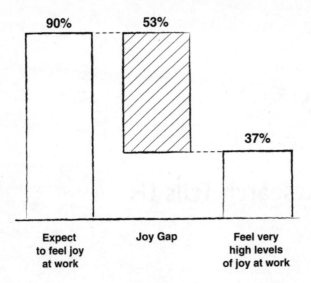

Figure 2.1 The joy gap at work.
Source: Kearney analysis 2018

We want joy at work. We hope for it. We expect it. But we're disappointed when work doesn't live up to our expectations. We call that disconnect between expectations and reality the "joy gap."

Our research revealed the following findings:

♦ **The joy gap affects people of all ages**: Baby Boomers, Gen Xers, and Millennials. And it affects people at all levels in the organization, from entry level to the C-suite.

♦ **People all around the world feel a joy gap.** This isn't a problem that discriminates based on where you live. Work cultures around the world are leading to less joy than we'd hope.

♦ **Older companies have the most work to do.** People who work at newer companies (companies less than 10 years old) reported substantially higher levels of joy than people from older companies. That distinction of joy felt by company age suggests that legacy companies have work to do. Leaders at older, established companies must be particularly diligent in cultivating joy.

The joy gap is growing

Three years later in 2021 (in the midst of the pandemic and social justice outrage), we ran a similar survey. This time, we found that the joy gap was still very present—and it was growing. The percentage of people who felt less joy at work than expected had risen from 53 percent to 61 percent. That's an eight-point increase over just three years.

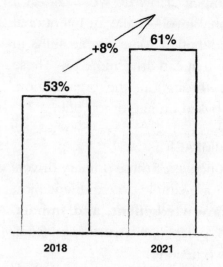

Figure 2.2   Joy gap, 2018 versus 2021.
Source: Kearney analysis.

Given the tumultuous and uncertain reality of the COVID-19 pandemic, it wasn't a huge surprise that people were feeling less joy at work than they'd hope. In 2021, organizational psychologist Adam Grant described the widespread feeling of being "somewhat joyless and aimless" and "languishing."[2]

---

[2]"There's a Name for the Blah That You're Feeling: It's Called Languishing," *New York Times*, April 19, 2021.

Even people on the sunniest end of the spectrum were feeling the squeeze. One of the most extreme changes from 2018 to 2021 was among people who report feeling the highest levels of joy at work. In 2018, 37 percent of people said they felt high levels of joy at work. In 2021, that number dropped 12 percentage points, and only 25 percent of people agreed with that claim. Even the most joyful people can't quite grab on to their joy.

We know what triggers joy at work

But this is a book about joy, not about despair. So how do we turn around these worrying numbers? How do we each—at a personal, team, and organizational level—make an intentional shift toward joy? Our research identified some simple shifts in behavior and company structure that can drive more joy. These "joy triggers" apply for people throughout the organization, without any notable difference based on age or job title.

HARMONY, ACKNOWLEDGMENT, IMPACT

In our initial 2018 joy study, we uncovered three primary drivers of joy. These basic "joy triggers" are simple: to experience joy, we need to feel **harmony, acknowledgment, and impact**. Together, they form the hallmark pillars of any successful team.

In other words, to feel joy, we need to:

- ◆ Be aligned and united with our teams.
- ◆ Feel appreciated for our contribution.
- ◆ Understand the purpose and power of our work.

We know that joy stems from believing one's work is truly meaningful. Employees who believe their "company makes a positive societal contribution" and who feel "personally committed to achieving the company's vision and strategy" experienced the most joy at work.

PEOPLE, PRAISE, PURPOSE

Our 2021 research identified three new focus areas for leaders who want to infuse more joy: people, praise, and purpose.

First: **People.** Given the stress, worry, and fear during the pandemic, people need social connection more than ever. We'll talk more about the power of people to drive joy in Chapter 3.

Next: **Praise.** We all want to be acknowledged for our efforts and results. We'll think about the link between praise and joy in Chapter 4.

And finally: **Purpose.** When we understand our "why," we can unlock the joy in our work. In Chapter 5, we'll think about how to link every person's work to the organization's broader purpose and help them personalize that purpose for their everyday work and context.

What's the difference between happiness and joy?

It's easy to associate joy with being happy. Having fun. Celebrating. Maybe that's why when we think about joy at work, we can brush off the topic as a fluffy "nice-to-have."

But joy is really much deeper than that. It's not just about fun or happiness. It's about having a stake in something you really believe in. Joy comes from experiences where you have a deep connection and a shared purpose with the people and the teammates around you. It's serious, it's substantive, and it's ambitious.

It's not too hard to imagine building a work culture that's fun. But building one that's joyful? That's another ball game.

We know what's holding us back from joy

This book is designed to be solution-focused. Forward-focused. Joyful! But I can't ignore the harsh reality: Most people aren't feeling joy at work. So while we're working toward positive change, we also must address the toxic, joy-killing norms we should all leave behind. If you want to shrink the joy gap at your organization, first let's look at what's blocking joy. What are the big obstacles you could move aside?

FEELING LOST AND WEARY

In our research, people cited excessive workloads and unrealistic expectations as their most pressing challenges and barriers at work. I see this burnout as a symptom of a more systemic malaise. In fact, many employees are clearly pushing back, noting that their managers are "militant" and unrelenting in pushing to get more done in less time. They seem adrift in the matrix of organizational silos and layers and victim to uncaring leaders.

We heard feedback such as this:

> "Sometimes, my job is too fast-paced, and I can't stop and think."
>
> "Work pressure and unrealistic targets are draining."
>
> "I feel stressed I'm going to fail because there is so much to do."
>
> "Upper-level management always pushes my team to do more in a shorter period. They never seem to be satisfied and keep asking more for less with each project."

As managers plan workloads, they should include a plan to avoid overwork and set clear boundaries. Have honest, open conversations about fair expectations. And map the work needs to a broader purpose and goal.

→ **TRY THIS:** What tools and strategies could you roll out to put barriers around work times? Could you plan "Focus Fridays" with limited meetings? How else could you realign work groups to make sure work stays manageable?

FEELING UNSAFE

Safety is physical, psychological, and social too. In pre-pandemic times, you might have assumed that most people felt reasonably safe at work. But the pandemic underscored real safety concerns, both in terms of physical protection from the virus and psychological safety from unfair treatment at work.

In our 2021 survey, less than half of respondents strongly agreed that their physical health and safety is reasonably protected at work. Less than half. That data point alone was alarming to us. Granted, this survey took place in April 2021, a time full of pandemic fatigue and disagreement about vaccine mandates. But even given the specific context of that time, no one wants to hear that people feel fundamentally unsafe at work.

And physical protection aside, it became clear that people also didn't feel emotionally safe at work. Less than 50 percent of respondents said they can be themselves at work. Organizations are not making employees feel protected or seen.

There's a real opportunity for leaders to address these basic human needs as a required precursor to joy. Especially in uncertain and challenging times, creating joy at work isn't just about throwing parties or celebrating the big wins. It starts with making employees feel physically safe, truly seen for who they are, emotionally supported, and inspired to do their best work.

It's worth noting that companies are increasingly being called on to take a societal role in their employees' lives. Work is no longer merely a transaction (time and effort for money). And in fact, the best workplaces were never transactional.

Again, leaders have the opportunity to provide human care and make sure people feel safe, seen, supported, and inspired.

> ***Follow your blisters.*** *Look for things that are fun for you, that you keep coming back to even if they don't come easily. What are the things that have had their hooks in you since you were a little kid? Follow those.*
> —Dan Cable, professor of organizational behavior at London Business School

SECTION ONE

The Three Drivers of Joy at Work

People, praise, and purpose are the three levers we can pull to create more joy in our own work and for the people around us. Let's spend some time digging into the research to illustrate exactly how people, praise, and purpose lead to joy.

CHAPTER 3

People

Our research showed an unsurprising driver of joy at work: the people we work with. People reported feeling joy when they were having fun and socializing at work. Those human connections aren't something extra or nice to have. They can drive overall job satisfaction and build trust on teams.

Think about the jobs from your past that you enjoyed the most. What do you remember about your work? For me, it's the people. I remember the teams. The collaboration, brainstorming sessions, after-hours teamwork, lunches, laughter, and conversations. My colleagues are my friends. My clients are my friends. I have always been a big fan of a team-based culture.

Maybe that's why I love sports. The connective power of joy is clearly visible in sports. When a team performs at its awe-inspiring best, overcoming its limitations and challenges, every player—indeed, the entire arena—experiences a brimming ecstasy that lifts the team even further. Success sparks joy. Joy fuels further success. Everyone is caught up in the moment.

As a leader, I think about our people and the culture they build with each other. And here's why: I know that **people** are our renewable energy source. If you don't motivate and energize people, you're not going to solve any of the big challenges your organization is facing or the problems we're facing in the world such as climate change and social injustice. No matter how much technology and automation you introduce to your organization, your core work likely is driven by **people**. And people—their feelings and their connection to their work and to each other—are at the root of building a joyful culture. Culture isn't some strategy that happens in a bubble. People are the spark who drive it.

In our surveys, people shared their memories of joyful moments at work:

> "When I was with my colleagues and we were doing a team exercise, we got along so well and had so much fun, we couldn't stop laughing."
>
> "We organized a secret birthday party for one of my coworkers. The smile and surprise on her face made me really happy."

Have you heard the saying that you are the sum of the company you keep? Well, we spend much of our time with our coworkers, whether that's digitally or in person. And if you feel joy at work, you are likely inspired by those coworkers. In our 2021 survey, 62 percent of the "joyful" (the people who feel the most joy at work) agreed that the people they work with inspire them. Among the "joyless" (the people who feel the least joy at work), only 20 percent agreed that their coworkers were inspiring.

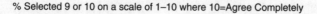

% Selected 9 or 10 on a scale of 1–10 where 10=Agree Completely

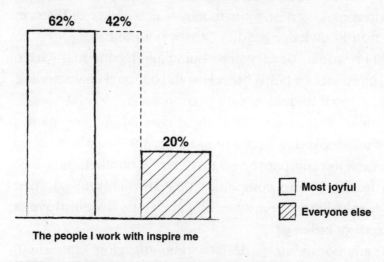

The people I work with inspire me

How much do you agree or disagree with the following statements about your current workplace?

Figure 3.1   Drivers of joy at work: largest gaps.
Source: Kearney Survey 2021.

Create belonging: It matters more than money

Enjoying your coworkers' company, building each other up, inspiring each other, and creating shared success seem to be *more* important than the numbers on your paycheck.

Jon Levy has been studying the way people interact for years. As a behavioral scientist, he spends a lot of time thinking about the mechanics of culture and connection. And he's seen a shift in how we all think about work, compensation, and our connections to the people we work with. His takeaway? For most knowledge workers, money is no longer the primary deciding factor.

"Research around income has shown that money doesn't generate significant happiness, unless you have instability around your next meal or where you're living," Jon says. "So if you're barely making rent, more money makes a huge difference. But for most knowledge workers, that's not the case."

In other words, once you're being paid enough to have stability, more money helps but it isn't the defining characteristic of whether you'll be happy with your job.

"We hear story after story right now about companies who've really looked at what compensation will it take to keep employees at the company? And there isn't a number," Jon says. Instead, he says, "The companies that are likely to succeed moving forward have to answer this question: **Do employees feel like they belong?**

"Not only does your work have to be engaging, interesting, competitive, and well-compensated; now (as fewer and fewer people go to church, synagogue, or mosque), the place of belonging needs to be the workplace. After all, we are spending more and more time there and employees, for better or worse, expect more from their company."

Jon's charge to organizations: Go all in on building belonging. Design your organization in new ways to create deeper connections where they currently don't exist. In the near future, he predicts, we'll see firms hiring "chief belonging officers" to invest in *belonging*, not just in HR as a vague discipline.

Dr. Ashley Whillans is a professor at Harvard Business School and author of the book *Time Smart: How to Reclaim Your Time and Live a Happier Life*. Her research supports Jon Levy's assertion that money does not equal happiness. "My research suggests that money has diminishing marginal utility for happiness," she says. "In fact, as we start to make more money, we become less happy because we start looking towards people that have even more money than we do, and we have less time to spend with friends and family or positively contributing to the community."

Ashley teaches her students how to think about trade-offs between time and money. "I see my students at Harvard Business School grapple with these trade-offs: 'How much should I work? How much money should I go after in my life?' I think it's really important to keep in mind that we do need to leave space in our lives to pursue both the work that we care about and the family commitments and the civic engagement, the community-building elements that are so important for happiness, both at work and outside of it."

Create connection points

Jon points to two phenomena that bolster connection on teams: vulnerability loops and the IKEA effect.

Vulnerability loops are how trust is created—through micro-actions of vulnerability. Here's an example of a vulnerability loop. Let's say Jon and I are talking, and he signals vulnerability (by telling me how he really feels or about something hard he's going through right now). If I ignore him or make fun of him or tell him to get over it, his trust in me is reduced. But if I support him, listen to him, and share my own challenges, I am signaling vulnerability back and closing the loop. The trust between us grows, and we feel safer with each other.

The IKEA effect is our tendency to disproportionately care about things that we constructed ourselves. It's a term coined by Dan Ariely, a professor of behavioral economics at Duke University. It explains why we value our IKEA furniture: because we have to assemble it ourselves. Jon says we could expand the IKEA effect to explain why we're more invested in relationships that we've been more engaged in building.

He encourages leaders to design work environments to trigger human connection—through vulnerability loops and the IKEA effect. For example, if you're holding a meeting to gather all employees, consider adding an interactive element. Jon suggests, "It might mean that we redesign town halls so that there are 20 minutes of conversation or speech and then 20 minutes of people going into breakout rooms to discuss how to move forward on things. And then the last 20 minutes would be people presenting ideas that they came up with. So now it's interactive. If we include interactivity and connection through breakout rooms or small groups, suddenly you're now getting more familiar with people across the company. You are bonding with people across divisions. We have to start designing interactions in a way that humans can actually interact and connect."

→**TRY THIS:** At your next virtual meeting, add a new interactive element. You might choose one of the following ideas:

- Build in time for unstructured, informal conversations that replicate the pre-meeting and hallway conversations of the office.
- Break into small groups, work on tasks on teams, and come back to the larger group to discuss.
- Find ways to add one-to-one connection even when you're meeting in a large group. Be intentional about setting up one-to-one virtual conversations to create the time and space for relationship-building.
- Use the full suite of applications and tools available in meeting software (chats, polls, etc.) to give large audiences and quieter participants flexible ways to engage.

Happy hours aren't the key to happiness

So how can leaders bring people together and create a sense of belonging? Jon Levy says happy hours (on Zoom or in person) aren't the way to go.

First of all, we know that culture isn't something relegated to after work on Friday afternoons. Culture is something woven into every part of your work.

And there are several specific reasons he advises against happy hours as corporate bonding:

♦ **The extroverts take over, while the introverts stay quiet.**

♦ **Happy hours center around drinking.**

"Considering the number of sober people that there are these days, that's kind of irresponsible as an activity. And drinking is falling out of fashion. People's relaxation habits and health conversations are changing," Jon says. He points to the explosion of nonalcoholic wine shops, mocktails, and a growing designation of "sober-curious" adults. While drinking increased in the height of pandemic lockdowns, global alcohol consumption has declined in the past 20 years.[1] If you're a Baby Boomer, the alcohol-heavy culture you experienced when you started your career just isn't as relevant or accepted today.

♦ **Happy hours don't actually create culture and connection.**

They're not interactive, and they don't create vulnerability loops. We don't necessarily build trust in these situations.

[1] Holmes, A. J., and Anderson, K. (2017). Convergence in national alcohol consumption patterns: New global indicators. *Journal of Wine Economics* 12 (2): 117–148, DOI: 10.1017/jwe.2017.15

Be a people-focused leader

We need these personal connections not just with peers but with leaders, too. The future will be forged by people-first leaders who show up authentically as themselves—and help the people in their firms fully grow and develop into their full potential.

Over the course of my career, I've watched the archetype for leadership change. When I started working, the standard leadership style was authority-based. Command and control. The archetype was the military, with top-down leadership. Senior executives commanded the loyalty of their employees and often devoted limited time outside of work to the issues that mattered most to them.

In the past few years, I've seen leadership become more empathetic, reflective, and authentic. These days, the old leadership style has been superseded by a new, values-based model, where the focus is on building followership and belonging by listening, rather than just talking. I call it *reflective leadership*.

You listen and learn. You share and apply what you learn. You're a force multiplier. You're not sitting in your tower, commanding your people. You're on the field with them, as an active participant. A player–coach. You're in the game.

My goal is to be a leader others want to follow. My goal is followership—creating an atmosphere where people are inspired and want to follow me, not because I'm in charge but because we believe in the same vision and have the same values.

But reflective leadership isn't easy. Leaders have to humbly acknowledge their own blind spots. Today's employees demand authenticity and accountability from their leaders. I have found that it's liberating to say openly, "I don't have all the answers."

I try to bring people onto my leadership team who complement me or even those who are antagonistic to me. I do that because I know my team and our decisions will be stronger when we bring in different perspectives. The Greek tragedies teach us that human pride is the source of most evils. Life will find a way of knocking you back to Earth if you think you have all the answers. The leaders I respect the most acknowledge that they're human. They lead with humility and open themselves to other people's guidance and input. They remember that they're part of a team, and they count on that team to keep them honest.

One person I know agrees with me: Dan Cable, professor of organizational behavior at London Business School and author of several books about human potential, including *Alive at Work* and *Exceptional: Build Your Personal Highlight Reel and Unlock Your Potential*.

"More than ever, leaders have to be really in tune with where each of their people is mentally, emotionally, even psychologically, in a way that we weren't as comfortable with, and maybe we weren't as demanding around [before the pandemic]," he says. He sees a rise in servant leadership. "Instead of being the dominant leader that has all the answers and makes the command-and-control decisions, it's more about the leader that tries to empathize with where each person is and then tries to help them get what they need to be effective at work. That's more of a servant role than a commander role."

He's encouraged by this trend toward vulnerable leadership. "I think the empathy, listening, and trying to be helpful as a leader are what we need, as opposed to the know-it-all, chest-beating, uber-masculine leader."

Brian Tippens, former chief sustainability officer at HPE, sees people-focused, authentic leadership as a must-have for companies going forward. The pandemic has wiped away any distinction of a separated "work" versus "life." Leaders' behavior needs to change, too. "Gone are the days where we think there's this bright-line distinction between our work lives and our personal lives. We have responsibility for acknowledging that our team members have fears and apprehensions. We are all bringing our whole selves to work in a way that we hadn't done previously. It's an equalizer."

Leaders have a key role in building joyful cultures by building connection with people, he says. "It's not a touchy-feely nice thing to do. It's how we drive business value. We can't get the business right if we can't get the culture right."

→ **TRY THIS:** If you manage employees, Dan Cable encourages asking them questions about more than their productivity. Open a vulnerability loop by asking: "How are you doing? How can I help you? What do you need from me right now? What kind of support would be useful?"

Think like a gardener and create "human magic"

Hubert Joly is a role model for me as I strive to be a joy-creating, empathetic leader. He led the consumer electronics retailer Best Buy through a major transformation from 2012 to 2019. He has also written a very good book about leading joy at work, *The Heart of Business: Leadership Principles for the Next Era of Capitalism*, which I heartily encourage you to read.

Hubert's work helps us remember that organizations are fueled by human energy. I think of joy as the life force of any team. He calls it "human magic."

He writes in *Harvard Business Review*:

Nothing grows in bad soil, no matter how good the seeds and water are. Similarly, no company purpose, regardless of how well it is defined, can materialize unless the company environment is fertile. A fertile environment is one where employees have a spring in their steps in pursuit of a noble purpose, and where everyone can become the best, biggest, most beautiful version of themselves. It is the kind of environment that can unleash what I call "human magic" and result in inordinately great results, like what we experienced at Best Buy as part of the company's resurgence.

What we had done was create an environment where employees were excited to express their untapped individual and collective potential.[2]

When Hubert took over the role as CEO of Best Buy, his financial goals were clear. But his success didn't come from "rational" actions, he says. Instead, he zeroed in on human magic. He focused on people. "I learned a long time ago that scientific, top-down management doesn't work," he says.

So instead of offering retail workers financial incentives to drive store performance, he says he focused on creating an environment with the core ingredients of human magic: meaning, authentic human connections, being seen and respected, autonomy, psychological safety, and a growth mindset.

And he fully credits that environment for Best Buy's financial turnaround. From that experience, he learned that the role of a

---

[2]"The Secret Ingredient of Thriving Companies? Human Magic," *Harvard Business Review*, January 10, 2022, https://hbr.org/2022/01/the-secret-ingredient-of-thriving-companies-human-magic

leader (in his case, the CEO) isn't to be the smartest person in the room. It's to be a gardener, making sure the soil is fertile so the seeds can grow.

Case study: How Best Buy doubled down on "human magic"

Hubert Joly, former chairman and CEO of Best Buy, tells a story about how human magic—and a little dinosaur magic—fueled business success.

One day in Florida, a young boy went to a Best Buy store with his mother. He was carrying a toy dinosaur, which he had received for Christmas. But the dinosaur was sick. The head had completely detached from the body.

The two employees who talked to the boy immediately understood what they had to do. Instead of just trading the boy a new dinosaur, they took the sick dinosaur behind the counter and performed a surgical procedure. They patiently explained the steps of their surgery to the child and eventually handed the boy a "cured" dinosaur. They delivered joy.

"Was there a standard operating procedure for sick dinosaurs?" Hubert asks. "Of course not. But they found it in their hearts to create magic. At scale, we have people who are doing magical things for customers and each other. That's a result of the environment we built."

*Everyone has it within them to be the change they want to see. **Lead from wherever you are** in the organization. Don't wait for a title.*

—Laura Lane, chief corporate affairs officer at UPS

CHAPTER 4

Praise

The second joy driver is **praise**. We all want to be acknowledged for our efforts, contributions, and successes. Leaders who are generous and specific with their praise build more joyful teams.

In our surveys, we heard about joyful moments of praise:

"When I was promoted within my department, all my colleagues gathered in my office to congratulate me and to celebrate it with me. I felt noticed for all the years of commitment I have made to the company as an employee."

"When our efforts and hard work are recognized by the higher-ups, it really fills us with joy."

In sports, praise comes easily. Great basketball coaches instruct their players that when they make a basket, they should point immediately to the teammate who made the pass or created the scoring opportunity. Acknowledging each player's contributions and cheering for each other powers the joy–success–joy cycle.

Praise seems simple: Tell people when they're doing a good job. Show your appreciation and respect. Reward hard work and progress toward goals. But our research about joy at work shows that specific kinds of praise—paired with other important elements such as autonomy and feedback—make the most impact toward creating joy.

Praise autonomous work

The first element to consider is **autonomy**. Praise is most meaningful when it recognizes efforts or decisions that employees have true control over. In contrast, praise for executing work that was highly directed or micromanaged is not as fulfilling.

It's therefore not surprising that whether someone agrees with the statement "I have control and autonomy over my work" is a strong indicator of how much joy they feel about their work. Among the least joyful, only 23 percent feel they have control and autonomy over their work. But among the most joyful, 65 percent feel a sense of control and autonomy.

When I think about autonomy, I think about the players on a rugby team. I'm a big fan of the sport, and I've never forgotten a key lesson that rugby players learn: You can get all the coaching and plans possible before a match, but when the match starts, there are no time-outs. You won't have a coach in your ear, drawing up your next play. It's up to the players on the pitch to make decisions and choices based on all the coaching they've received up to that point. The team trusts and empowers each player to execute the game plan.

I think about rugby players when I think about preparing teams to go out into the real world ready to make tough decisions and represent the firm. The goal is to prepare them, then trust them to do good work on their own—autonomously.

When I interviewed professional rugby player turned coach Andrew Suniula, he reminded me of the player autonomy in the sport. "Rugby empowers players to make decisions," he said. "You don't tell them what to do, but you give them boundaries to operate and be themselves because that's why you chose them and put them in that position."

How could we all think like rugby coaches, empowering others to make good choices?

→ **TRY THIS:** Praise creative actions.

To increase your team's joy, try recognizing the work, outcomes, or decisions that people made independently, without firm guidance from a manager or teammate.

Let's say Alisha, a sales rep, filled out her expense report on time, as is required. That might not warrant a celebration. But if Alisha excelled by winning over a customer who had tough objections or challenges, going above and beyond to find a creative solution on her own, it's time for praise. Seek her out, and recognize her efforts.

Pair praise with feedback

We also found that high-praise cultures can be fertile ground for working through honest, constructive feedback. It might seem counterintuitive, but praise is a prerequisite for developmental feedback. Because feedback can feel threatening, employees are more likely to hear feedback if it's delivered in a supportive, positive culture built on trust. If I believe that my manager genuinely cares about me, my personal growth, and my well-being, then I'm more likely to hear, value, and use their constructive feedback.

Focus on the quality of praise, not the quantity

Effective praise is sincere and specific. Quality matters more than quantity. If employees perceive that praise is insincere, placating, or condescending, it can do more harm than good. Insincere or superfluous praise feels manipulative and erodes trust instead of building it. If you're going to praise someone's work, be specific and heartfelt.

→ **TRY THIS:** Take 20 minutes a week to share specific, sincere praise.

Praise individuals, not just groups

Our research shows that giving praise to individuals is important, and it's also important to praise teams.

At an organizational level, praise must be twofold:

- ◆ Recognize and appreciate the hard work, efforts, and dedication of the entire team.
- ◆ Distinguish and reward the exceptional achievements of high performers.

In other words, directing praise to a broad group isn't enough to create moments of joy for individuals. Think about how you'll praise groups *and* how you'll create moments for discrete praise to individuals and small teams.

→ **TRY THIS:** Praise individuals, not just teams.

- ◆ Praising a group is not enough. People want leaders to acknowledge their *individual* actions. For leaders, that means being attuned to what each employee is doing, paying attention to their efforts and needs, and creating moments of real connection to acknowledge those efforts and build trust over time.

Encourage people to show appreciation for their colleagues

Finally, praise has the power to drive joy—but not just when it comes from your boss. Recognition from our teammates and colleagues means a lot, too. Who doesn't want to feel appreciated?

Our 2021 survey showed that 61 percent of people who feel high levels of joy at work say their colleagues express genuine appreciation for each other's contributions.

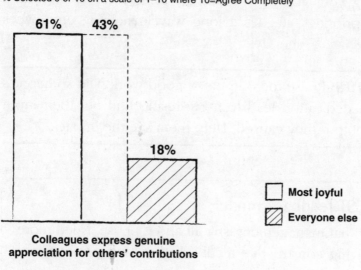

% Selected 9 or 10 on a scale of 1–10 where 10=Agree Completely

61%   43%

18%

☐ Most joyful

▨ Everyone else

Colleagues express genuine appreciation for others' contributions

How much do you agree or disagree with the following statements about your current workplace?

Figure 4.1   Drivers of joy at work: largest gaps.
Source: Kearney Survey 2021.

Build a culture where everyone freely and generously shares praise when they see good work.

→**TRY THIS:** At your next meeting, ask your team: Who has helped you this week? Who has kudos to share? Build people up, and encourage a spirit of team appreciation.

Use praise to underscore impact

In the next chapter, we'll talk about the power of purpose in the quest for joy at work. But it's important to note that praise and purpose go hand in hand. Dr. Ashley Whillans, a professor at Harvard Business School, has researched the power of recognition in the workplace. Her finding: Praise is more powerful than financial incentives, especially when people can see the specific, tangible impact of their work.

"When you help employees see how even the simple things that they're doing on an everyday basis are shaping the world or helping your company move the needle on its important business priorities, it goes a long way in helping employees feel appreciated," she says.

→**TRY THIS:** Praise the outputs of good work. Did someone's energy or dedication lead to a big result? Call out their input *and* the output they caused. Help them see the impact.

The BEST feedback model

I know that management isn't all about praise. Need more help giving constructive feedback that feels positive, not belittling? My firm has developed a model to give the "BEST" feedback. It's all about collaboration, listening, and a focus on improving.

Behavior: Identify the observed behaviors with examples.
Effect: Describe the effect the behavior had/is having.
Shared conversation: Jointly listen, acknowledge, and discuss with an open mind.
Takeaways: Define what you've learned, and make a plan for action.

*When I was a kid, my mom used to tell me: 'If you're sad, troubled, or anxious, **start giving thanks. Be grateful.** You will find joy through suffering. It's joy as a practice.'*

—Callie Field, president of T-Mobile's
business group

CHAPTER 5

Purpose

The third driver of joy is **purpose.** People have been thinking about purpose from the earliest days of philosophy. We're all searching for our "why."

In our survey, we heard moments of joy tied to purpose, whether it was helping customers:

"When I can help customers and make them happy, that brings me joy."

helping teammates:

"I love to guide younger members of the team to go from no knowledge to leading professionals."

or living up to their own potential:

"I feel joy when I find an innovative solution to a problem."

Purpose is the "why" of an organization's existence—the driving force and the bond that brings the organization together to achieve success. Over the past decades, purpose has evolved from a focus on profit and shareholder value to the broader influence and impact an organization can have to effect positive change.

Paul Polman, the former CEO of Unilever, observed that people "don't want to look back at what they've done and say, 'Well, I built the market share of Dove 4.5 percent. . . .' No, they want to say, 'I helped so many millions of women achieve self-esteem. I helped so many people improve their nutrition levels, and in doing so, I've actually strengthened the institution I represent.' And that is really purpose in action."

Michael Nyenhuis leads UNICEF USA, a nonprofit with the clear purpose of helping the world's most vulnerable children. "Purpose is what gives us joy in life," he says. To him, purpose is "engaging in something bigger than ourselves."

Understand your *ikigai* (a reason for being)

To understand the idea of purpose in our work, I often turn to the concept of *ikigai*. Rooted in Japanese culture, *ikigai* first emerged during Japan's Heian period (794–1185). It has no direct equivalent in the Western world, at least not one that can be neatly captured in a single word.

Derived from *iki* (meaning "alive" or "life") and *gai* (meaning "benefit" or "worth"), *ikigai* was conceived as a way to help individuals achieve fulfilment by finding their purpose and reason for being in life. Any of us can apply its principles to benefit the teams we work on by identifying the sweet spot where our passions and talents converge with the things that the world needs and is prepared to pay for.

Ikigai is about doing what we love doing, doing it well, and focusing on only those things that we have the power to control. In our fragmented modern world, *ikigai* offers us a compelling way to break down the walls we've built to separate our

Figure 5.1   *Ikigai,* from the Japanese concept of "a reason for being."

personal values and the values that make our organizations tick, a way to find our purpose and translate it into meaningful action.

At my firm, we use another way of thinking about *ikigai*: the X Model. The X Model is all about finding the intersection of personal success and your organization's success.

Here's what it looks like:

In the X Model, we're striving for moments at the intersection of what you care about, think is important, and are good at—and what the organization more broadly cares about, thinks is important, and is good at. We call them "apex moments" or "punch the air moments"—the times when for a minute, an hour, or a day, you're applying your core strengths toward values you care deeply about in service of something that is meaningful to you and others. That's when real joy happens.

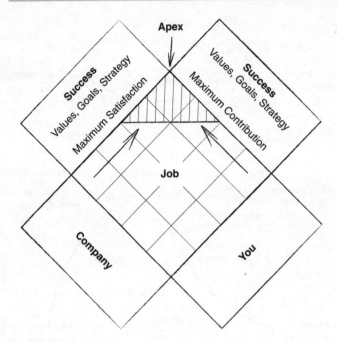

Figure 5.2   The X Model of engagement.
Source: BlessingWhite

And in other words, if you can't find the overlap between what success means for you and what success means for your organization, your work won't be sustainable.

Find your zest

I'm not sure I've ever met anyone as joyful and optimistic as Dan Cable, professor of organizational behavior at London Business School. Dan has dedicated years to studying the human push toward purpose.

"The brain wants you to understand your cause and effect in the world," he says. "It wants you to understand what your strengths are so you can make a better impact and get more resources." When we follow those urges and understand our *ikigai*, we can tap unto what Dan calls "zest."

"Zest means life starts to feel like an adventure that you *get* to do instead of a hassle that you *have* to work through," he says.

Dan pointed me to an image in W.H. Auden's series of poems *Horae Canonicae:*

> You need not see what someone is doing
> to know if it is his vocation,
> you have only to watch his eyes:
> a cook mixing a sauce, a surgeon
> making a primary incision,
> a clerk completing a bill of lading,
> wear the same rapt expression,
> forgetting themselves in a function.
> How beautiful it is,
> that eye-on-the-object look.

"How beautiful it is, that eye-on-the-object look." This poem makes me think of the Cirque du Soleil performers in my current hometown, Las Vegas. They are so fully engaged in their art, performance after performance. You can see in their bodies that their work lights them up.

Dan feels that way when he's teaching. "You're so within it that you're still discovering it. You're learning it again," he says. "You're at your best. You're lit up." It's that state of flow, of energy, of zest. It's joy.

Rethink the corporate purpose statement

But when we try, with the best of intentions, to corporatize that human quest for zest, all of the life force and personality can fall away. Over the past 10 years or so, "purpose" has started popping up in the mission statements and brand identities of most major corporations. Many companies are now homing in on the idea of purpose, striving to define and communicate the reason for their existence.

Dan is watching how the concept of "corporate purpose" has moved from an organic movement to a manufactured way to appease employees, and he's seeing a trend: "Company CEOs know that they should be cooking up a purpose statement. But that's really not how it works." In other words, there's no purpose statement that will replace intrinsic motivation. And you can't just manufacture purpose.

"For purpose to work, it has to be something that lives in your emotions," Dan says. "You have to be able to see it and respond to it. How do you make it feel like it's something that affects you, day in and day out? How do you make it part of the work?"

Granted, it takes an enormous amount of sustained focus to answer (and keep answering) the question, "Why are we here?" Jon Levy suggests a simple approach to crafting a corporate purpose that starts with employees: Communicate your purpose in a few simple words. Everyone in the organization needs to understand it. "Unless you can easily communicate in a few words what you really want to do and be honest about it, it's going to be hard for employees across the company to get behind it," he warns.

Mind the gap

When you promote a corporate purpose but don't translate that purpose into tangible action, you create a "purpose gap" between what you say and what you do. It's a gap between intention and action. That gap looms large and can create an unforgivable chasm in employees' and customers' minds.

My firm's Purpose Quotient Index research shows a troubling gap between a company's purpose statement and how much *actual* progress employees see toward that purpose. Employees and customers have little patience for companies that proclaim a purpose but don't back it up with action. The next generation is looking to business leaders to actually act. They're not interested in mere words; they want to see how we're going to make it happen.

Earlier in this chapter, I introduced the idea of *ikigai* in terms of our personal purpose as individuals. But we can also think about *ikigai* in terms of our collective, broader purpose as an organization. Crucially, *ikigai* gives organizations the opportunity to take a step back, reflect, and reassess their true purpose rather than pursuing progress at any price. Companies are living, growing organisms—and that purpose evolves as they develop. If you have a gap between your stated purpose and your organization's *actual* actions, it's time to step back and reassess either your purpose or your actions toward it.

Personalize purpose

Importantly, having one overarching purpose for the organization isn't enough to drive individual joy. The real magic comes from personalizing that purpose. Align everyone's work to the greater purpose so they see they are making a difference.

Everyone has a song inside of them. How do you make sure they can sing it within the context of their work?

How do we link corporate purpose to the individuals who are carrying it out? How do we help people connect the dots between the bigger purpose and the emails they send, spreadsheets they make, or customers they serve? Dan Cable says the key to putting corporate purpose into action is personalizing it. Help people see who they personally impact every day.

His advice: Help people find a story or a narrative about who's affected by what they do. They need to understand their own purpose, not a leader's narrative about purpose. For example, maybe Merck's corporate purpose is "We build better, stronger lives." But for a Merck employee in accounting, their personal purpose is "When I put these budgets together better, the decision-makers can make better decisions about saving lives."

Here's how to help people understand their personal purpose: Ask them two questions.

1. Who would you say your customer is?

In Dan's experience, many people in the corporate world are stumped by that question. If someone is external facing, they know who their customer is. But what if they're in accounting? Of course, they still have customers. Who are the people who use their work?

Then, ask an even more powerful question:

2. Who is your customer's customer?

Think about the person you serve who uses your work. Who are they serving? You could probably serve them a lot more effectively if you knew that.

If they don't know the answer, give them a month. Tell them to think about it, make some calls, ask some questions. Their charge: Try to learn about your customer's customer.

"The idea is to help people link what they do all day to the lives that are affected by the work they do," Dan says. "It's a way of seeing your impact on other human beings. They might be inside the company. They might be outside of the company. But they are human beings that are affected by what you do all day long."

"When we have that narrative and we believe in that story, it starts to ignite us. And that's when we get the dopamine and we get charged. When we have a sense of purpose—why I do what I do—we're more resilient in pursuing that end."

In other words, leaders can help people see the impact of their work so that it's woven into their job as opposed to being a generic slogan.

Harvard Business School Professor Ashley Whillans points to research that even when people are working on tasks they really don't like doing, such as data cleaning or a rote monotonous task, they tend to feel much better about it and feel like their jobs are more meaningful when they know that their work is helping their colleagues get their work done.

She shares an example:

> Job crafting, which entails using imagination to redesign one's job without the involvement of management, is one technique that connects an employee's everyday work activities with the organization's purpose. For instance, a hospital cleaner may reframe their work as helping sick people instead of simply cleaning. Or an insurance agent might reframe their work as getting people back on track after an accident rather than processing paperwork.[1]

Here's my realization: I've learned that I can't ever really understand someone else's "why." I just have to make it possible for them to realize it. And for many of us, our own "why" is undiscovered territory. We haven't had the time or the space to explore it because we're so busy getting our work done. What if leaders made that the next frontier of work: prioritizing self-reflection and self-awareness?

---

[1] Daniel Stein, Nick Hobson, Jon M. Jachimowicz, and Ashley Whillans, "How Companies Can Improve Employee Engagement Right Now," *Harvard Business Review*, October 13, 2021, https://hbr.org/2021/10/how-companies-can-improve-employee-engagement-right-now

Case study: How two companies think about purpose

If you work for a toy company, what's your purpose? Is it to drive corporate earnings? Or could it be to bring joy to children?

UNICEF USA President and CEO Michael Nyenhuis talks to a lot of corporate leaders about the connection between their work and their purpose. He has seen that the most joyful organizations understand their purpose. "Employees want to know that they're engaged in work that produces social good, that's about a larger social purpose in the world," he says.

He shares two examples:

Toys or joy?

A major toy company went through a mindset shift. Instead of thinking about themselves as a manufacturer of toys, they thought of themselves as an organization whose purpose was to bring joy to children.

Leaders at the toy company realized that mental health issues for children around the world are huge and too often unaddressed. One of the key ways to address children's mental health is through play. People at the company started to look for ways to create opportunities for kids to feel joy.

→**TRY THIS:** Ask yourself: How does my organization's work bring life, opportunity, or joy to the people we serve?

French fries or a brighter future?

A family-owned business owned multiple fast-food franchises. The owner shared stories of employees from immigrant families who started at an entry-level counter-service job in a restaurant and are now store managers, creating new opportunities for themselves and their children. The owner realized that the purpose of the company isn't just to make fast food but to provide meaningful employment and opportunity for thousands of people.

→**TRY THIS:** Could you look at your work differently? What ripple effects does your organization have on people's lives?

Think about how your everyday work contributes to the ***larger social good***.

—Michael Nyenhuis, president and CEO of UNICEF USA

SECTION TWO

Joy in a Post-2020 World: How to Create More Joy

Many people around the world think of 2020 as a dividing line between the "before times" and the "after times." In the second half of this book, we'll consider the reality of life after 2020, in those "after times."

But before we think about all of the implications of 2020—the pandemic, the fight for social justice, and the sudden move to remote work—I want to offer a different perspective on 2020.

On January 25, 2020, people around the world celebrated Chinese New Year, a day that signifies renewal and rebirth. And this one was especially meaningful, because 2020 was the start of a new 60-year cycle—composed of 12 lunar years times the five elements (wood, fire, earth, metal, and water). It heralds a new beginning and a unique pivot point in human history: a new cycle and a year of reckoning.

There's a magnitude and mysticism about the number 60 that threads through many cultures. It's right there in the origin of mathematics with the ancient Sumerians and Babylonians. Related to that, it's how we measure the passing of time: 60 seconds in a minute, 60 minutes in an hour.

The year 2020 was always foreseen as heralding a tectonic shift, as 1960 did before it. And yes, it certainly delivered. But it's not just about COVID-19. It seems like all catastrophes converged at once. The continuing fear that puts knees onto necks and razor wire between children and their parents. The persecution of individuals and groups for being the "wrong" shape, size, color, gender, race, religion—you name it. The 30 million people who still live in slavery, here and now, in the 21st century. The death warrant hanging over our planet. It's like living in a science fiction movie where the only thing that's certain is uncertainty. I call it the "no normal."

Perhaps more disconcerting is that 60 years ago, the issues weren't so very different. I was a baby on my mother's lap on the plane from Taiwan to the United States as my parents sought a better life. The Cold War across those straits and others was intensifying. We worried about being minorities in the deep South, the first sit-in protests against segregation took place, and it wasn't safe—or legal—to be in a same-sex relationship in many countries. What has changed?

We've seen what we're capable of when it really, truly matters. We build hospitals in days. We move entire workforces and business models online. We develop pandemic-curbing vaccines in a matter of months. We collaborate on a global scale to share expertise and go after new solutions.

Call me superstitious, or fanciful, but maybe the ancients were on to something, the universe is speaking to us, and there's a reason why we landed this throw of the dice. Maybe the next 60 years are our chance to right some of the wrongs, to reconcile and reckon. This is a moment that we must meet, and all such moments determine how we look at ourselves. What type of world do we want to leave behind us? What type of world do we want our children and theirs to inherit?

Here's to doing our part, for the next 60 years and beyond.

CHAPTER 6

Joy in the Hard Times

Post-2020, we're living and working through more disruption than anyone planned on. For so many reasons, it can be hard to keep your head above water, much less swim toward joy.

How do we find joy in the hard moments?

During the pandemic, two professors at Harvard Business School created a class about leadership and happiness. They used the course to guide business school students through the spring of 2020, a time of major uncertainty and unhappiness for many. I later heard them present about the core lessons they'd shared with students. Here's one that stood out to me: **Keep your line in the water.**

The tides are changing very quickly right now. It's hard to know which way is up. You might want to throw up your hands and retreat. Give up. But they suggest that we should do the exact opposite. Professor Arthur Brooks says we can use these times of tide change to learn, grow, innovate, and thrive: "With a shift in mindset, we can make transitions into a source of meaning and transcendence," he writes in the *Atlantic*.[1]

"The best time to catch fish is during a quickly changing tide," he says. "Practically the only mistake you can make is not to have your line in the water."

In this chapter, I'll share ways you can keep your line in the water—to lean into the current environment of disruption, change, and confusion and welcome what's coming next, even if you can't control it.

Embrace change

Gerri Elliott led sales and marketing at the tech giant Cisco during 2020. She says the most important strength for a leader is the ability to adapt and embrace change and discomfort. "This pandemic has changed industries forever," she says. "Retail, education, medicine, transportation, travel, they've been changed forever. But we, as leaders, have to embrace that change."

She points to her favorite saying: "We cannot direct the wind, but we can adjust the sails." Gerri says it's a helpful reminder that she can't control everything.

"I can only focus on what I can control and let go of absolutely everything else. It keeps me grounded, keeps me calm, and in the present."

→**TRY THIS:** Take a quiet moment to reflect. Ask yourself: What is stressing me out? What is blocking me from feeling joy in my work?

Make a list of your biggest stressors and concerns.

Then ask, Which of these things can I control?

---

[1] Arthur C. Brooks, "The Clocklike Regularity of Major Life Changes," *Atlantic*, September 10, 2020, https://www.theatlantic.com/family/archive/2020/09/major-life-changes-happen-clocklike-regularity/616243/

Strike through the items on your list that you can't control. Focus on what's left, and let the others go.

Accept that failure is inevitable

When you're navigating a period of change, you'll have to make tough choices. Some of your decisions might be the wrong ones. You'll have to take risks.

That was true for Stephen Tang, who led the medical testing company OraSure during the height of the pandemic. In 2020, the company was called to quickly develop new tests for COVID-19. He says OraSure needed a culture that fostered innovation. But the team also needed to "understand and accept that failure is a valuable experience."

"Failure is certainly valuable when you're trying to create something that's never been done before," he says. "Risk and failure go hand in hand. There's no progress without risk. There's no risk without failure. And I don't think we're fully alive as people or as an organization unless we dare to stretch ourselves and grow beyond what's comfortable."

Acknowledge your mistakes and get real

Callie Field has held several leadership roles at T-Mobile. She built her career at the company in sales and distribution, but she didn't have much experience in customer care. She describes taking on a new leadership role and being out of her element.

"When you step into something you haven't known before and try to make strategic decisions, you don't always understand the implications of those decisions," she says. In the early days of her new role, she changed the way call center employees managed and measured their calls with customers. It didn't go well.

"As a new leader, I had to pull my team together and say, 'I really messed up. I need to understand where this went wrong, and I need your help. Here's what I was trying to accomplish.'"

When she owned her mistakes, admitted she was wrong, and humbly asked for help, she was able to build trust with her team and turn things around. She focused on dealing with the problems at hand, without the cloud of ego or embarrassment getting in the way. Her team knew: No sweeping problems under the rug. Let's deal with them openly.

Plus, they learned how to disagree. "We learned how to have conflict, how to fight, and how to tell each other the truth. I think that's really important for a team that wants to innovate, take risks, take chances, and solve problems together."

That early failure helped Callie build trust and cohesion on her team quickly. She credits the failure for shaping her team's core dynamic. Instead of earning an early win as a new leader, she navigated an early failure—and came out as a stronger team because of it.

Later, during the pandemic, the culture of "real talk" proved to be valuable. "I've always tried to have an approach where our teams can tell me what's broken or what's stupid," she says. When teams were working remotely during the pandemic, Callie started having those "real talks" over virtual town halls, and she would bring in other leaders whose attention or help they needed.

Meeting remotely with teams around the world meant that conflict resolution could happen virtually, and quickly. "If they're having a tough time with some of their counterparts in retail, I just pull the leader into the virtual town hall meeting. They don't have to get on a plane. There's a new level of accessibility and transparency. We threw all the pretense out the door. We're here, we're in this, we're trying to survive in our personal lives, and we're trying to go after these audacious goals as a team. Let's just get real with each other."

Have the courage to be a beginner

For the most fearless among us, joy at work is all about learning.

Why do I say "fearless"? Well, let me ask you a question. What have you learned so far this week?

It might take you a second to come up with an answer. You've probably read a lot of emails and had a lot of conversations about work. Maybe you read some news articles to try to make sense of what's going on in the world. But what have you learned that's actually *new*? Have you made yourself vulnerable or put yourself in a situation where you weren't the smartest person in the room?

Learning is so important for us as humans. Learning new things, figuring out new challenges, taking in new information— it's what makes us feel vibrant and alive. And at work, it's what keeps things interesting. If we think about that old archetype of the command-and-control leader who has to know the most about everything, we don't have much space for learning something new. But if we open ourselves to the humble experience of being a beginner, we create the opportunity to grow. We're eager to keep learning. We're lifelong students.

Kathryn Parsons knows a lot about the humbling experience of learning. She started the technology education company Decoded with a simple goal: teach people to code—in a day.

Why? Kathryn knows that people see coding as a confusing, mysterious digital world. Her mission: take a subject matter as vast and seemingly complex as coding, and condense a year's worth of learning into a single day. Demystify it, take away all the jargon and clichés, and put it in someone's hands. Make it a safe place to play, learn, and grow. Lower the stakes. Create an accessible learning environment where it's okay to fail.

Kathryn's work focuses on decoding fast-moving technology, but in the process, she's also decoding workplace culture. Her job is to create a safe, welcoming space where people can ask stupid questions. During the pandemic, her team led trainings on the basic building blocks of technology, where people can ask, "What's the cloud?" or "How do I change my Zoom background?" She's seen CEOs lead the way, humbly admitting, "I don't understand this. But I want to learn."

"It takes a lot of bravery to learn something new," she says. It's hard to feel like a novice. When people feel comfortable and safe, they can admit that they don't understand something and give themselves the freedom to explore and fail.

Companies need to create a culture of brave learning. Kathryn points to studies that predict large majorities of current job roles will be replaced by machines in the near future. "I think we need to flip the dialogue on that research," she says. Instead of anticipating that half of the workforce will become obsolete, we should be encouraging people at all ages and in all roles to keep learning, growing, and transforming. People can learn new things and transform into a future version of themselves. Through her work, she has seen "transformative learning stories" that prove the power of learning.

Millennials have already experienced the need for continuous learning, Kathryn says—and she includes herself. "Millennials are the anxiety generation. We're told there's no career stability, we're going to be working until we're 90 years old, and we should expect to have 30 different careers in our lifetimes." While that kind of message might drive anxiety, it also drives learning. "Millennials are sponges for learning," she says. "They're the first person to leap on board" when new employee learning programs are offered.

"For me, joy at work is being in a learning environment. Every day, I want to feel like I'm acquiring new skills that allow me to solve problems better. Learning isn't something that takes you away from work; it's something that is just an intrinsic part of the work that you do," she says.

"If you want to attract the smartest, brightest, most ambitious Millennial talent to your organization, you need a culture where lifelong learning is celebrated and encouraged," Kathryn says.

Take time to reflect

Hubert Joly, former CEO of Best Buy, is a reflective leader I admire. He describes the Great Reflection that many leaders experienced during the darkest days of the pandemic. "During COVID, when you couldn't go outside, you had to go inside and ask: How do I want to be remembered? Do I want to be the person who increased the share price? Or do I want to be remembered for how I touched people? Or how I took on societal issues and moved the needle?"

Hubert says that "going inside" and reflecting didn't always come naturally to him. "For many years, I made the mistake of having my head cut off from my body. But as leaders, we need to lead with all our body parts: head, heart, guts, eyes, ears. The spiritual life of a leader is essential."

Double down on purpose

In tough times, it can be hard to see the bigger picture. Laura Lane is chief corporate affairs officer at UPS, a company with a clear purpose that seems designed for our recent global tumult: "Move our world forward by delivering what matters."

Laura is eloquent and wise. When I spoke to her after a hectic two years, she told me she's been reflecting on the impacts of the pandemic. As she thinks about all of the challenges the world has faced, she feels optimistic. "I've seen nothing but resilience. I've seen innovation. I've seen people rising to the challenge and reaching out to one another and reinforcing the power of the concept of all of us being stronger united.

"From that vantage point, I actually believe this pandemic has allowed us to be a little bit more reflective and maybe appreciate more about what brings us together than what divides us," she says. "And I'm really hoping that we tap into those learnings and help find the solutions for all the challenges that we've seen play out on the global stage over the past year and work together to build that better world."

On the day I talked with Laura in March 2022, she was closely monitoring a new crisis: the war in Ukraine. She told me about the teams of UPS employees around the world who were pouring themselves into providing help and supplies to Ukrainian refugees—"delivering what matters."

When you're facing hard situations on a personal level, in your organization, or at the global scale, it can be hard to tap into joy or hope. But Laura says her team asks: How can we spark joy? How can we show people how to make a difference? How can we help employees control what they can control and deliver what they can? She describes creating momentum, one tiny step at a time.

For example, UPS leaders put out a call for supplies to be sent to refugee centers. Twenty-four hours later, UPS employees had donated 60 pallets of supplies and prepped them for delivery. "You have to tap into the good that fundamentally exists in people," she says. "We need to help people be purposeful, not immobilized by despair. If we give people a purpose-driven action they can take, we show them they can make a difference."

Laura's work and leadership is inspiring to me. She reminds me that even in dark times, we can each choose to be a light. Business can be a platform for change, creating positive ripple effects.

Her words of advice to anyone who's feeling overwhelmed by all of the hard things happening in the world: "When sh— happens, shine."

Keep chasing your goosebumps

Finally, if you're in a low moment in your career or you can't find work that brings you joy, Callie Field offers the "goosebump test."

"I've definitely had times in my career where I hated my job," she says. "I found it completely uninspiring, or I worked for a really difficult boss that I didn't believe in or admire. It's hard to find joy in those times. I would say to anyone who wants purpose and joy in their careers: if what you're working on doesn't give you goosebumps, if you can't get excited about it, don't stop until you find that thing. Do the things that give you goosebumps."

Ken Davenport shares the same advice from his office on Broadway. He's an actor turned Broadway producer who has spent decades watching how creative people find joy in their work. His main takeaway: When work stops being fun, it's time to tap into your gratitude—or time to make a change.

"It's as simple as finding joy in what you do and loving what you do," he says. Even Broadway performers don't necessarily have a mile-a-minute, glamorous work life. They're showing up to put on the same show eight times a week. And if they're in the chorus or ensemble, they're not belting out solos; they're doing their best to blend in with the person next to them. They have to find ways to keep the joy in their work. "It is exceptionally hard," Ken says. "They have to work really hard to remember, 'Wow, how grateful I am to be on Broadway. So few people get a chance to do this,' and find ways to keep it fresh every single night."

And if you can't access that joy, he says you should get out, and find something that you *will* enjoy. He says the most successful people he knows have made a transition at some point in their careers. Maybe they decide they don't want to perform on stage eight times a week anymore, so they pivot into choreography or directing or leave the industry completely. But they push themselves to make a change before malaise or discontent starts to infect their happiness. And that lesson applies to anyone, whether you're clocking in to work in an office or showing up to rehearse on Broadway.

Think like an apprentice and look to your mentors when times are hard

One of my core priorities at Kearney has been encouraging apprenticeship. Consulting has always been an industry driven by an apprenticeship model. People with more experience train and teach the next generation, and the cycle continues. I see apprenticeship (and, from the other side of the relationship, mentorship) as a primary way to create a joyful, generous, inspired culture. In fact, I included it in my core platform as a leader. My focus on DIAL (diversity, inclusion, apprenticeship, and leadership) centers apprenticeship as a key way to move forward.

We think of mentors as "talent stewards" who help their mentees reach their full potential through feedback, coaching, and building trusting, meaningful relationships.

When times are hard, work doesn't feel joyful, and your path forward isn't clear, try thinking like an apprentice. Ask yourself: Who could help me? Who has something to teach me? How could I learn and grow? Mentors can transmit joy and passion. Find your mentors and ask for their help.

Find ways to have fun, even in the boring or hard parts of your work. **Life is short,** *and if you're not having fun in the process, you're not going to be successful in your mind, your heart, or your bank account.*

—Ken Davenport, Tony Award–winning Broadway producer

CHAPTER 7

Safe, Seen, Supported, Inspired

As I've shared, the pandemic changed the tenor of my conversations about joy at work. Suddenly in 2020, I was having emotional conversations with other corporate leaders and my colleagues. People were ready to get real, to drop the act, and to connect in a more personal, raw, authentic way.

And from all the research that is coalescing about how people feel about their work, it's clear that people need work to be a place that's safe for them, even when they're vulnerable. We all want to feel safe, seen, supported, and inspired.

Creating a safe workplace (physically *and* emotionally) is not a far-off dream or a nice-to-have for only the most progressive employers. It's a baseline requirement.

Safe

START WITH PHYSICAL SAFETY

I'll repeat the troubling statistic I mentioned earlier: In our 2021 survey, less than half of respondents strongly agreed that their physical health and safety is reasonably protected at work.

We assume that answer was heavily influenced by the fear and alarm of the pandemic, but it also flagged a major concern that extends beyond the pandemic. If people don't feel physically safe, they'll never relax enough to feel emotionally and psychologically steady. Put physical safety of the people in your organization before anything else.

SUPPORT MENTAL HEALTH

My friend Crystal Ashby is a lawyer and corporate board member with more than three decades of leadership success. I talked with her when she was the president and CEO of the Executive Leadership Council (ELC), a membership organization for Black executives.

As the leader of ELC during the pandemic, she asked: "How are we making sure that people are okay emotionally? That their mental health is being cared for?" She was attuned to what was going on with her team members, and she noticed when something felt off.

At my firm, we've also been thinking a lot about how to be stewards of mental health for our people. Even before the pandemic, it was becoming increasingly obvious that the consulting world had some major issues to address. Stress levels were going up for consultants, leading to more leaves of absence and, ultimately, people leaving the industry. But when COVID hit, those concerns about mental health became very clear. It pushed us to accelerate our mental health support. We have partnered with a nonprofit called Unmind to roll out new strategies, including mental health assessments and training a team of "mental health ambassadors" inside the firm who are trained to spot mental health concerns in their peers and start conversations about helping them.

These strategies and tools are all incredibly important, but we also need to think about mental health in a new way that removes the stigma around mental health issues. Mental health is a spectrum that we're all always navigating, just like we're navigating our overall health. We all have "health" all the time. We just have different flavors, versions, and qualities of it. And by the same logic, "mental health" is not something bad. It's something you *have*. Sometimes, you have poor mental health. But we tend to talk about mental health as only a negative, as opposed to a spectrum. Just like our physical health, we need to manage our mental health all the time.

We are committed to:

◆ Improving the way mental health is perceived, openly discussed, and more vigorously supported in our firm.
◆ Sharing lived experiences and raising awareness to normalize the fact that it is okay not to be okay.
◆ Providing resources, tools, and training to support our people with their mental health.

And finally, it's not just up to individuals to manage their mental health. Organizations and employers have a huge role to play, and it has to start in the actual structure of the work and the culture. Kearney Chief Human Resources Officer Stephen Parker agrees. "We know that we can't solve on Fridays the mental health challenges that we ourselves create Monday through Thursday," he says. "If your organization is driving loneliness or stress, your mental health workshops on Friday afternoons aren't going to work. If that's what we're doing, then we're getting nowhere. You can't put icing on a cake that is flawed. We need to regularly take stock and ask how we can remove barriers that are keeping people from doing good work and being fulfilled in their jobs."

AS A LEADER, GO FIRST

Changing the atmosphere and making people feel safe and protected is all about showing up and leading with vulnerability. During the pandemic, we've seen leaders having courageous conversations and showing up authentically. I call it the "unmasking" of the executive—and really, the unmasking of everyone at work. Senior leaders have abandoned their armor to show their full, complex emotional truth. And teams have started to acknowledge and unpack the challenges, trauma, and loss we've all experienced during this difficult season.

Stephen Tang led the medical testing company OraSure through the intense months of the early pandemic, as the team there rallied together to rapidly create new COVID-19 testing. He quickly felt the pull to have more vulnerable, honest conversations with his coworkers. "In the normal course of business, I don't think I would have been so eager to share my own personal journey. But under the circumstances, I've learned to make myself more vulnerable. I've tried to invest in learning better about relationships and about myself." The result of that new openness? New emotional depth and connection at work, even in the especially tough year of 2020.

To feel safe, people need to feel confident that they can show up as themselves and receive "unmerited grace" (a term I'm borrowing from Bryan Stevenson, author of *Just Mercy* and executive director of the Equal Justice Initiative)—a basic respect for their raw humanity, even if it doesn't align with the organization's goals or the typical workplace narrative. And when you extend that grace and create a safe, supportive space for people, their outlook, potential, and joy start to truly blossom in a deeper and longer-lasting way.

Seen

EMPATHIZE WITH HOW PEOPLE ARE FEELING

Most leaders have not faced a pandemic before. I know I hadn't led a global team through a pandemic. When I talked with other executives in 2020, I wanted to know how they were making tough decisions. How were they keeping people physically safe and emotionally steady?

Gerri Elliott was leading sales and marketing at Cisco during 2020. She remembers how the Cisco leadership team prioritized employees' health concerns early in the pandemic. "When the pandemic first hit, we knew that folks had questions about the disease and concerns about the spread." So very early on, the company had an all-employee virtual meeting with the company's medical doctors and health workers to answer questions. They gave 24 hours' notice, and 36,000 people showed up to the meeting.

The feedback was so overwhelmingly positive that it became a weekly meeting called the Cisco Check-In. "We just checked in with people," she says. "How are you feeling? How's it going? What questions do you have?" The meetings were medically oriented in the beginning, but as the Check-Ins evolved, leaders realized that people needed a break. They needed some joy, so they brought in entertainers to sing a song or talk about their work. The entertainers also shared how vulnerable they were feeling, and the questions they were working through. The Check-Ins continued to evolve in the summer of 2020, and after George Floyd's murder by police in May 2020, the Check-Ins were focused on hard, open conversations about race and social justice.

Cisco also introduced an all-employee off day called "A Day for Me" for employees across the company to take a break. The reaction from employees was gratitude. "You would have thought that we gave everyone a million dollars," Gerri says. "The gift of that day was so important that we're doing it once a quarter now." She describes an influx of messages, photos, and stories from employees who wanted to share what they did on A Day for Me: "I visited my mom for three hours in the nursing home." "I went fishing. I reconnected with nature."

I asked Gerri how her leadership has evolved after leading through a pandemic. She says she's learned just how important it is to be empathetic and listen to the people around her. "Everyone is fighting a battle you know nothing about," she says. "That hit me during this pandemic because everybody is dealing with something. I go into meetings now remembering in the back of my mind that folks might feel like they have the weight of the world on their shoulders and their plates are overflowing. I always felt like I was empathetic, but this has taught me that everybody deserves a little unmerited grace."

Gerri's experience helps me remember that, often, our challenges and troubles are invisible to other people. Empathy is an antidote to that invisibility.

CREATE AN ENVIRONMENT THAT FEELS INCLUSIVE

In 2020, when I talked with Alicia Tillman, who was CMO of the global technology company SAP at the time, she was focused on building a work culture that felt *safe* for everyone.

"When you create environments where people feel comfortable expressing themselves, you begin to realize how much more connected than disconnected we are as human beings," she says.

Creating a culture of safety can help improve feelings of inclusion, too. "Inclusion is about creating a safe space for people to connect based on their beliefs and values. Often, diversity and inclusion are dealt with in terms of hiring a diverse workforce and putting goals in place based on the number of women you hire or the number of Black employees you hire. But it goes so beyond numbers and ratios," she says. "It's so much more about how you can create an environment that's based on shared values."

When you're leading a global organization, geographic diversity is also crucial. That's why Alicia made a major decision to extend the sense of diversity and inclusion in her organization. In 2020, she realized that the global leadership team she helmed didn't have the right representation of people from around the world. "I oversee marketing for the entire company and all of the 180 countries in which we operate. We needed to be more cognizant of local nuances" instead of just US norms, she says. She changed the makeup of her leadership team to do that.

Once her team included people that were actually representative of all the regions where the company operated, she saw a shift in the team's dynamics and the effectiveness of their decisions. Specifically, she saw employees adopting new global standards more readily. "If my Greater China team recognizes that their leader was part of helping to shape the standards, they are more willing to embrace and adopt them because they know that their needs have been taken into consideration. Whereas by contrast, if my entire leadership team is based in the US and they're developing standards that get rolled out all over the world, there's going to be reluctance to accept that. The general perception will be that none of the local cultures or nuances were taken into consideration."

In other words, the decision to diversify the team making the decisions helped employees all over the world feel seen.

Supported

ACCEPT AND SUPPORT PEOPLE AS THEY ARE

UPS has gone through some major cultural changes in the past few years under the leadership of CEO Carol Tomé. Laura Lane, the company's chief corporate affairs officer, says the changes were about empowering employees to be themselves at work. "I'm firmly committed to being a part of that change in our culture that makes work not drudgery, but joyful," she says.

Here's what the company did: "For us, it's been about listening to our people and hearing what would make them happier coming to work. Across the board, we've heard that people want to bring their authentic selves to work," Laura says. "So that's meant, if you've got a tattoo, show us your ink, wear it proudly because that's an expression of who you are. Come as you are. When people feel like they're empowered and encouraged to be themselves and bring all of their great ideas, I think they're happier."

UNDERSTAND WHAT WORK IS LIKE FOR OTHERS

Callie Field inspires joy in the thousands of employees in her orbit. In 2020, as chief customer experience officer at T-Mobile, her job was all about joy.

Nearly 20 years ago, Callie started her career at T-Mobile in a very humble way. She was looking for jobs after she graduated from law school, and after what felt like 100 rejections, she started to pay the bills by selling cell phones from a cart in the mall. I'll let her tell you about it:

"When I say mall cart, I don't even mean the kiosk. I mean the cart: the thing that you have to chase around and go find where your job location is. It was the holiday season, and my boss had a penchant for sales employees wearing costumes. So I found myself in an elf costume selling cell phones. That wasn't the life that I thought I was going to have.

"I say all that, one, because it's funny, and two, it was pretty humbling. And I think that's a good place to start when you're thinking about joy. Because learning how our products translated to actual customers and figuring out how to have fun and be successful from the ground up was really important to me. And it has helped me be a more connected, authentic leader today."

I relate to Callie's story. My first job was at McDonald's when I was 16, so I understand starting in a humble place.

Callie learned how tough it is to work directly with customers. "I learned how challenging it is to be on the front line and stay on top of all of the price changes, product changes, customer sentiment, and how things actually work on the network. I really learned the ins and outs. And today, our call center employees have over 21,000 documents that they are responsible for knowing and accessing. I got to experience the complexity of that kind of job firsthand."

ACT WITH A SPIRIT OF SERVICE

Callie knows the power of support from a strong mentor. She still remembers one moment with her second-grade Sunday school teacher, Nedra. "She pulled me aside, put her hands on my shoulders, and very lovingly said, 'You are so special, and you're going to do great things with your life.' I have never forgotten that, not ever. It was powerful for me. I felt that I had a special role to play in this world. I can think of times when I was not being kind to myself or when I was really not making great decisions and how that moment was so alarmingly powerful to remember.

"If you've had people that believe things about you and push you to be more of that person they know you can be, that is an unbelievable, almost indescribable gift."

She thinks about that moment with Nedra when she talks to people who are just starting out in their careers. "I try and look around my team, our company, and say, 'How can I be that for those people?' When you get to serve somebody that way or love them or help them engage with their life differently, that's better than a paycheck. That's better than a title or an accomplishment. It makes my soul expand."

Her advice: "Don't be scared to love people. I have found that people have a deep need to be cared for and respected. To care deeply about your employees and to create business solutions that reflect a deep love and care for employees is actually an unbelievably powerful tool. So invest and take a risk. Maybe you love someone or care about them, and they completely screw it up, and it's a mess, but it's worth it."

One of the ways Callie sees love enacted at her organization is through benefits that transform employees' lives. "More than 80 percent of our frontline employees haven't completed college. And an even higher percentage are the first people in their family to go to college. We offer a free tuition reimbursement program and measure how many of our employees complete their education and encourage them to do so in the fields of their choice. Because investing in themselves, their own confidence, their ability to think through difficult problems, not only for customers but in their professional development, has created a lot of value in our organization." She sees tuition reimbursement as an opportunity to change the trajectory of a family's life. "That's really motivational for me," she says.

Inspired

I said at the onset of this chapter that in order to experience joy at work, we need to feel safe, seen, supported, and inspired. Let's talk about inspiration.

Feeling *inspired* by our work is, honestly, a little new in the corporate context. A cynic, or someone who is holding tight to old ways of thinking about work, might tell you that inspiration is for artists and poets. But corporate workers? They need to feel inspired, too?

And again, I'll return to my question: **Why would we settle for anything less?**

Millennials are often called "spoiled" for expressing that they're looking for meaningful, purpose-driven, *inspiring* work. I'm not a Millennial, but I raised three of them, and from being their dad, I know that they want to be supported and inspired. They want to be treated with respect as individuals.

If you want to inspire people, you need to create a culture that is aspirational. Dan Cable of London Business School helped me think about inspiration in a new way. People aren't an empty bucket waiting to be filled with knowledge, he says. People don't learn through a process of "here's the set of facts, and now we give them to you." Instead, he says, "education is about inspiration. The same is true of work. Work is not just getting the process done. It's also about feeling engaged enough that you want to find out how to make the process better or how to solve a problem within the process."

And finally, if we want inspirational work cultures, we need to make sure that the people in charge are able and willing to inspire. Former Best Buy CEO Hubert Joly says that the most important decision you can make at a company is who you put in a place of power. He remembers meeting with senior leaders at Best Buy. He was explicit about the leadership philosophy. He put all of the company's values on the table—adages such as "Make employees your North Star" and "Admit you don't have all the answers." Then he told the leaders in the room, "If you don't agree with these principles, no problem. But you can't work here."

Case study: Measuring joy as a business metric

T-Mobile has a unique story. As a disruptive, challenger brand, the company's business strategy is all about putting the customer first and breaking norms in the industry.

T-Mobile Business Group President Callie Field describes how the company's leadership changed the way they thought about customer service. Instead of tracking traditional call center metrics such as "average handle time" and "call efficiency," they swapped in more meaningful metrics for the customer. They decided to measure joy. "Are our customers happy? Are they staying longer? Are we deepening our relationship with them, and are we helping our customers to do all of that with less effort?"

They looked at similar metrics for employees—the people on the other end of those conversations with customers. "We said, 'Let's hold ourselves accountable for the employee experience just like we are the customer experience. Are our employees happier? Are we deepening our relationship with our employees? Are we creating less effort for our employees?' That led us to a business model that created new rules for customer care. We fully empowered our teams to have all the permissions and tools to get to resolution the first time to make it right. And we put our people on teams that reward and recognize and motivate each other to do the right thing for the customer, so there is no handing off or hiding accountability.

"We're going to love our frontline. We're going to lean into them. We're going to believe with all of our hearts that no company can match what this company can do because of our people. And we're going to make our decisions around those people. We're going to invest in them by making them all shareholders in the company. That creates a lot of trust and authenticity.

"And that's been very liberating for call center employees not to be looked at as a unit cost of doing business, which is how most companies look at customer service. Instead, they're looked at as the heroes and champions of the brand, who should be put on center stage and listened to."

---

*Understand what matters, and **don't sweat the small stuff**. Listen to each other, lean on each other, and care for one another.*

—Alicia Tillman, former CMO of SAP

CHAPTER 8

Virtual and Hybrid Work

The *way* we work now—where we are, what tech we use, how we communicate with each other—has completely changed for many people since the pandemic started. The whole world has telescoped, and everything is topsy-turvy. Our definition of work, the workplace, the workforce, and the worker are all in flux.

Some aspects of remote work are challenging, and we'll explore those challenges in this chapter. But for the leaders reading this: Don't try to go back to "work as usual." There is no old way of working.

As Decoded founder Kathryn Parsons told me, "The cat has been let out of the bag. It's not realistic to expect people to come 'back to work' exactly as they did before. People have embraced a new way of living and working. And the best talent are going to join companies that reflect how they want to work." In other words, if you're doubling down on commuting into the office for a 9–5 workday every day, you might want to reconsider what your workforce really wants and needs.

Overall, Harvard Business School professor Ashley Whillans thinks the pandemic will make a long-term positive effect on the workplace. "Our younger generations are pushing on workplaces to care about aspects of our personal lives that workplaces were never set up or designed to do. We used to work in factories, produce a certain number of widgets each day, and go home. Workplaces look nothing like that now, and they're going to continue to look nothing like that in the future. It's going to look more like the freedom and flexibility model that younger generations want."

Instead of going back to the old ways, I see an opportunity to embrace new conversations about what we all want from work. Kathryn Minshew, co-founder of career development platform The Muse, has her finger on the pulse of what the next generation wants from work. "The fact that everything has been turned on its head has allowed people to ask really big, important questions about how we want to be working," she says. "And more broadly, what norms and standards about the way that work gets done should we consider changing?"

Be aware of how remote work is different than in-person work

For all its benefits, there's a lot we miss out on when we don't see our coworkers in person. Ashley Whillans sees major challenges for younger workers who may miss out on learning and mentorship. "It's harder to have these hallway conversations, these informal social interactions where you're getting to meet colleagues, you're learning about your job, you're sense-making after an important meeting," she says. A remote-only workforce could lead to "a lot less understanding of what the heck just happened in that meeting because we're not having those hallway conversations, not overhearing our manager make sense of what just happened."

Plus, when we meet digitally, we lose a lot of the contextual elements we subconsciously pick up on when we get together in person. We can't see body language or physical cues: the poker game of a meeting.

And we miss out on connection. Remember the "vulnerability loops" that Jon Levy explained to us in Chapter 3? They're harder to create when we're virtual. "In a workplace where we're face to face, those vulnerability loops can happen really fast. I can whisper something to a coworker during the meeting. We can have a private joke. That's a vulnerability loop. Digital platforms aren't designed for them," Jon says. Instead, people often feel isolated and overwhelmed on digital platforms. They don't feel seen by or connected to the other people on the call.

Finally, virtual meetings are one-directional. One person is presenting. Everyone else listens. It's much harder to have a spirited back-and-forth over a video call. Why does that matter? Jon Levy says it's all about influence. He uses the example of a basketball game. Attending the game in person is a very different experience than watching on TV. "In person, you have a sense of influence. You can scream, you can shout, you can cheer, you can clap, you're part of the action." When you're at home, you can't.

I know I miss the dynamic conversations that can only happen in person. There's no replacement for the spontaneous anarchy that happens when people are together in a room. You learn, you disagree, you cut people off. Zoom makes every conversation much more ordered and polite, and I think we miss some of the zing that comes from a feisty in-person discussion.

Make conscious decisions about where you'll work
Remote isn't the answer for everyone or every kind of work. There are many benefits to seeing people face to face or working

on a project in the same room. The key is to make a conscious decision about the best work format for any given situation, instead of defaulting to always in-person or always remote.

IN PERSON

As you think about how and where you'll work, consider the best environment for different kinds of work. Heads-down, focused work might be best at home if you have a quiet home work space. Important meetings, collaboration, and brainstorming might be best in person, gathered with your team. Cisco executive Gerri Elliott shared good advice with me: use in-person time for the "moments that matter." Serious conversations, big celebrations, hard decisions. Those are the moments that matter.

REMOTE

One real benefit to remote work? It cuts down on the pollution associated with commutes and travel. "Climate change is at the forefront of younger generations' minds, so corporate travel is something they're going to push up against," Ashley Whillans says. Most people didn't travel for work for at least a year, she says, and they saw that work was still possible. So they'll be asking whether they *really* need to go back to a hectic every-week travel schedule. "I think we're going to see a lot of employees push against the formal and traditional ways of doing things," she says. Heavy work travel "infringes on our ability to take control over our time—and negatively contributes to the environment."

Her advice for leaders? "We're going to need to be a lot more strategic with our decisions around travel [for work]."

HYBRID

Ashley Whillans has been studying hybrid work and its implications for all of us. She has a word of caution about hybrid work: "This is one area where we have to be very careful. Hybrid is going to pose some particular challenges."

When some people come into the office and some don't, there's a risk that "some people are going to be left out of conversations that might be crucial for mentorship, for innovation, for creative ideas." Leaders will be asking: How do we make the hybrid environment equitable and inclusive?

Find new ways to build connection

As I shared in Chapter 3, *people*—our social connections—are vital to feeling joy at work. Grinding away on the computer at home day after day can make work start to feel like a transaction. "Rather than learning and stretching, it's about getting it done on time, moving it through the process. Rather than it being a spontaneous interaction in the hallway, it's grinding through another three hours," Dan Cable says. "Zoom calls can be efficient and transactional, but I wouldn't call them *fun*."

To combat that transactional feeling among faculty and staff, Howard School of Business dean Anthony Wilbon says he has made a conscious effort to invest in more social activities in order to keep the culture alive. Team lunches, grand celebrations around events like graduation—they're more important than ever.

"My concern when I think about joy at work is that the dynamics of this environment have changed so much." The culture has shifted dramatically. After two years of working from home, he wonders, "How much enjoyment are people really getting?"

Our teams at Kearney have been thinking about how to keep the culture and connection alive. It may be harder to host huge gatherings with colleagues from around the world, but we can get small local teams together for lunch. Remembering to invest and schedule that time for human connection, face to face, is going to be important as we move into the future.

More joyful meetings

People around the world are trying to figure out: How can we bring more joy to our work meetings?

The best answer is simple: Have fewer meetings. Eliminate the bottom 70 percent of them. Give the ones remaining a clear purpose. This is liberating.

No, really. The research backs me up. People overwhelmingly want less meeting time in their work day. Here's a novel innovation. Give the people what they want. Free up time to do what really matters. Try getting rid of at least half of your meetings and measure if your teams are still as productive.

I used to try to explain to my parents what management consulting is or does. After years of rational explanations (I do top secret work for companies and countries; I help people and clients reach their full potential) leaving quizzical looks on their well-meaning faces, I eventually caved and simply explained, "I go to meetings and send invoices. If the customer likes them, they pay me." They nodded with some reassurance. That explanation made sense to them, because they assumed what many people do: Meetings are where people agree and where business progress happens. But is that really true? I think not, and you know not.

And if you *do* need meetings, let's make them meetings that matter. Make them just a bit more memorable.

Joyful meetings:

◆ Have a clear purpose—a "so what?" for the meeting.
◆ Are about listening to each other, not talking over each other.
◆ Give people a chance to authentically connect.

- ◆ Allow people to be spontaneous and go off-script.
- ◆ Help team members get in sync with each other.
- ◆ Make sure everyone knows their role, much like in a pro team, Broadway ensemble, or a jazz quartet.
- ◆ Create a sense of excitement. People are surprised or feel anticipation.
- ◆ And, most importantly, joyful meetings give people their time back!

Rethink how you measure performance

Anthony Wilbon says he's been rethinking what he measures from employees. "The focus has to be on results and output," he says—not just input like how much time someone works or whether they're at their desk when you walk by. He says that people are changing their focus from time spent to outcomes achieved. Managers should be asking: What are you giving me as a work product? What is your output? What are the results? That represents a major change for some leaders, he explains. "Some old-school managers are going to have to adapt how they evaluate people."

Stay open to change

It's also important to note that a person's or an organization's decisions about remote versus in-person versus hybrid work may continue to evolve. The pandemic has taught us that we're all facing many factors we can't control. Don't hold your decisions about where you work too tightly. Be ready to flex and pivot without strife when the next major change event rolls around or when you hear feedback from your team that work isn't working.

Ashley Whillans agrees: "We're going to go through a period of fits and spurts. The hybrid model is going to be challenging.

We're not going to get it right the first time. I think we're going to need to rapidly experiment, test, try out new ways of working, be willing to fail. I think that what the younger generations will really bring to the table is this appetite for experimentation."

Finally, I'll share the most important leadership lesson I learned from the "fits and spurts" of the pandemic: You have to resolve at some central character level that you can't control everything. You can't remove all of the uncertainty from any situation. As a leader, I have learned to focus on the things I *can* control: how I communicate, how often, to whom, and what I say.

I also learned to be very deliberate in taking time off work. I turn off the video calls, I shut off my email, and I go for a jog every day. I learned that being a role model during times of stress is as important as being a role model in good times.

Focus on what you can control, and let go of absolutely everything else.
> —Gerri Elliott, former chief sales and marketing officer at Cisco

CHAPTER 9

Social Justice and Joy

In the past few years, since we started studying joy at work, we've seen themes that started out small and increasingly grew bigger, like Pac-Man. We started with joy at work. But joy led to justice, mission, purpose, and sustainability.

Even as we continue to see the bitter evidence of endemic injustice, there is hope for the future, and there is human aspiration. There will be great joy in achieving true justice and equity.

In this chapter, we'll think about the relationship between social justice and joy. My view: You can't even begin to think about joy until you have a baseline sense of justice. My message: There will be no joy without justice.

As I mentioned in the introduction, I think of the fundamental ABCs as allyship, belonging, and culture. They lead to each other. And the more these three things are harmoniously and authentically executed, the more teams can take on big challenges. Having a strong team changes everything. It steels you against challenges, and it primes you for joy, even during hard times.

Let's think about how we can drive more joy, starting with justice.

Joy and justice for all

WHO DESERVES JOY?

First, I want to share a fascinating conversation I had with Ingrid Fetell Lee. Ingrid is a designer who is known for her exploration of joy. She wrote a book called *Joyful: The Surprising Power of Ordinary Things to Create Extraordinary Happiness*. When I first met her in 2019, well before COVID was a possibility in anyone's minds, we had a lovely conversation about the psychology of color and joyful design.

But we also touched on the complex nuance of joy at work. Who deserves joy? "We feel like we have to earn joy," she told me back then. "And we earn it by working to deserve it. Some of that has to do with our Protestant work ethic: the inherited belief that we work and work and work in this life, and we earn joy in the next life."

Ingrid's reflections resonated with me. I grew up in a Chinese household that also emphasized delayed gratification: work before play. You can't go out to play until you finish your studies.

And when I called Ingrid again in 2022 to see how her perspective had shifted since the pandemic began, I found that this idea of earning or deserving joy was very much top of mind for her.

Ingrid told me that the pandemic has pushed her to reexamine her own relationship with work, joy, and purpose. And remember, Ingrid is someone who finds a lot of joy in her work. She wrote the book *Joyful*! "My work is incredibly filled with purpose. I do find tremendous joy in my work. I love what

I do," she says. The tension comes from her very present sense that not everyone is able to access that kind of joy at work.

She wasn't afraid to question the core premise of this very book. "It's problematic to expect that everyone should be able to find joy in jobs that were not ever created to be joyful and under working conditions that are not very humane," she says. Before the pandemic and her own Great Reflection, she says that she thought of joy at work as an individual challenge: how can we all find more joy in our jobs, and how can employers help employees find more joy?

She used to give keynotes to companies about joy, and at the time, she framed joy as a way to improve retention. "It was a productivity strategy," she says. "How do we keep workers happy and make work a place they want to stay and continue to work?"

But now she sees joy at work as a more systemic problem: We have an unhealthy relationship with work. "We have an economy that is not grounded in humanity," she says. "We saw that with COVID. We had to send people back to jobs that weren't safe or healthy so we could keep the economy running. But what's the point of keeping the economy running [if we're not protecting the humans in that economy]? We're all reassessing the role of work in our lives, and it's not something I thought I would see. I know my own priorities have changed, and it's been a profound realignment."

"Joy isn't a strategy," she says. "It's a right."

She has realized that the American focus on work leaves little room for joy, or even for life outside of work. "The centrality of work in the American consciousness really pushes life aside," she says. "There's work, and then there's everything else. And as a result of the pandemic, a lot of people are realigning their lives to say, 'Is work actually the center of my life? Or is it one of the many aspects of my life?'" That realignment can take some pressure off work, Ingrid says. She's interested in a shift toward a culture where work isn't our primary source of purpose and meaning.

I appreciate Ingrid's perspective and her challenge to my way of thinking about joy at work. And what I hear from her is that joy is the goal for all people. Joy is a right. Work isn't the only way to find or earn joy. But from my perspective, we each have the opportunity to move our own work toward joy. Can we have our cake and eat it too? Can we build successful organizations that create joy instead of squash it?

WE NEED TO INCLUDE EVERYONE

Let's go further. I've shared that I have always found ways to play, have fun, and socialize at work. I think of my own work as play—my playground. It's why joy and work are so closely connected for me. But when I mentioned that perspective offhand to Ingrid, she flagged the inherent tension I was excluding from the conversation.

She and I have work that feels like play, she says. But is playful work really achievable for everyone within an economic system where we have to work to survive? "There are a lot of jobs that are not playful," she points out. "And they're often the worst compensated jobs."

But joy at work—and play at work—isn't something that people only deserve when they hit a certain salary tier, she says. "I don't think joy is a privilege. Finding joy at work is a problem that everyone in society is struggling with. But we often talk about joy at work as a problem that's just for professional workers in offices when, in reality, there's a whole larger segment of the population that do work that we're not talking about. Joy isn't something that you only get to have once you work your way up to a certain level. The desire and need for joy in your work is universal. This topic of joy at work is hugely important right now because people need and want it. But we need to include everyone."

How do we push "social justice" into the mainstream of business?

Even if we agree that we all deserve joy, there are a lot of external factors that make joy hard to come by. There are seemingly endless tragedies swirling around us in the world: death, war, racism, hatred, natural disasters, climate emergencies. And each tragedy seems to pound us with the inconvenient truth and realization that we still have so very far to go to create the preconditions for joy and justice. There's a lot of work still to be done to eliminate intolerance, biases, blind spots, and violence in the communities that we're inextricably a part of.

How do we find joy and justice in this broader context? How do we keep the faith and keep fighting?

I hold on to hope and focus on what I believe and what I can influence as an individual and leader. We can all inspire someone. We all have the power and specific levers that we can pull to lead change and maybe drive a new narrative and a new story.

The question I ask myself every day is, "How will I use my power and influence today? What will I stand up for? Even in a hurricane?"

There's a real need for leaders to acknowledge and engage in the broader conversations about justice that are rising around us. How an organization responds to pressing social issues such as Black Lives Matter, the gender pay gap, and LGBTQI+ equality has a direct impact on employees' ability to access joy. To move the needle on joy, we need to have hard conversations about justice.

SUSTAINABILITY: BELIEVE IN THE POWER OF ESG

In the old days of business, there was a naive belief that businesses could just focus on doing well inside their four walls. When I talked with Hubert Joly, former CEO of Best Buy, he told me that the old way of thinking doesn't work anymore. Instead, every business leader has to think about their interdependence with their community and the world. "The role and scale for leaders has changed," he says. "It's not just your four walls that you have to think about anymore. It's all stakeholders."

My friend Brian Tippens is a leader with many years of experience guiding major companies to become more diverse, inclusive, and sustainable. He has helped me think about how we can all take our vector (our force and direction) and multiply it to create joy in the corporate world.

He was at HP Enterprise for 20 years with various roles, including chief diversity officer and chief sustainability officer. He has helped me have more than one aha moment about environmental, social, and corporate governance (ESG).

Brian says that broadly, we think of ESG as the "nonfinancial" factors that affect a company's performance. But in recent years, ESG seems to have a direct tie to financial numbers. For me, that means that talking about "social" justice isn't some far-off, fluffy conversation that's somehow separate from the core work of the business. As Brian points out, ESG and "social" work is threaded through every part of an organization.

Brian's roles expanded the traditional definition of sustainability. He has overseen all of the social elements that the company touches: carbon impact, diversity and inclusion among employees, building a sustainable supply chain, paying living wages to everyone along that supply chain, and addressing human trafficking and modern slavery.

He sees more and more companies creating roles such as chief sustainability officer and chief purpose officer to bring together all social causes. And ideally, they report to the CEO: they're a core business driver, not a siloed function off to the side.

Corporate sustainability and social responsibility are transforming very quickly right now, and Brian feels that changing tide: "Everything's changing as we speak," he told me. "We wouldn't have been having the same kind of conversation just two or three years ago. Before, this was all an afterthought. So it's good to see so much attention being paid to the space." He expects consumers and governments to only strengthen their scrutiny of companies' social practices in the next few years, making his job extremely important, with a direct impact on the business. "We're tying sustainability to the broader corporate strategy," he says. "Every company is going to need a business case for sustainability."

What drives Brian to do this challenging work? "I've always been naive enough to think I can change the world," he says. "I'm drawn to roles that support 'doing well by doing good.' And sustainability is a space to really focus on that because it's around driving positive change with a purpose. And if done right, it really helps to enable the business success."

I see a huge opportunity to change the conversation in companies toward more sustainable practices and more social justice. ESG leaders have a chance to be a force for good and a multiplier of impact. I see leaders like Brian who are committed to doing good and moving the needle. Brian's example of leadership for good brings me major joy.

RACIAL JUSTICE: A TIME FOR RECKONING

My friend Crystal Ashby spent the summer of 2020 in her hometown of Detroit, taking care of her elderly grandmother and her mother, who had contracted COVID-19.

Being with these women, who had fought for their rights in the past century, gave her an opportunity to reflect on their stories—as they all watched a new story of racial injustice and reckoning unfold on their TV screens.

"They lived through riots," she says, and now they were watching a public reckoning over George Floyd's murder by police officers. "My grandmother used to say that we had an obligation and a responsibility to make sure that people listened this time because this time was different. We were all quarantined at the time that this happened, so we were all attached to our devices. We weren't seeing it replayed on the news. We were watching it being filmed live."

Here's what was going through her head in the summer of 2020: "You look at a situation like COVID-19 that adversely impacts the African-American community, and then you pivot to a situation where a man gets murdered and, for the first time after I don't know how many murders, everyone in the world stops and says, 'Okay, wait. There's something wrong here. There's something really, really wrong.' And it's not just in the US. The world has stopped. And then you say, 'So how do you turn this moment into a movement?'"

Crystal advised corporate leaders during that summer of reckoning. She cautioned them against expecting their Black talent to be the ones in charge of explaining what was happening, sharing their own context or stories, and building a path forward for reconciliation. She'd say, "They're tired. Their guts have been ripped open, and they come to work and you say to them, 'Explain this to me. Help me understand.' How do you go to the victim and ask the victim to help you understand something?"

A key problem in corporate America is basic representation. Crystal has the data to illustrate the challenge: "In the Fortune

500, there are only four Black male CEOs.[1] [Black people] make up 14 percent of the population. And then if you extrapolate out and you look at C-suites, you look at corporate boards, the seats are very, very small. So what's the rationale for that?"

And how do we move forward in a more diverse, accepting, just way? What reckoning needs to happen inside our organizations?

ACKNOWLEDGE THE CURRENT STATE OF JUSTICE AT YOUR ORGANIZATION

If you don't start with reality, you can't fix anything. I've talked with countless people who told me that the first step to understanding and improving the injustices happening in their organizations was to stop, listen, and acknowledge the (sometimes ugly) truth.

Howard University School of Business Dean Anthony Wilbon says that acknowledging reality means "really understanding and being honest about the history of this country as it relates to race and inequity and injustice. We can't be in denial about how horrible the history is with Blacks and whites and Asians. We have to be real about what white privilege is and what oppression of African Americans has been and accept it. I think there's a sense of denial because people think that it happened 200 years ago," he says. "The fact that it's in the past and we try to ignore it is not going to help us. There has to be an open dialogue. There has to be a very direct intent on finding solutions that help us move forward. Otherwise, we're just going to keep repeating these cycles. These crisis

---

[1] Vanessa Yurkevich, CNN, June 2, 2020, https://www.cnn.com/2020/06/01/business/black-ceos-george-floyd/index.html

situations are going to keep happening. It's an ongoing dilemma that we have to really put our arms around, and it starts with the basic, honest conversations."

Callie Field did just that at T-Mobile. "The first thing I had to do was create a safe space for underrepresented groups, people of color, and specifically Black employees to talk about racist experiences they had at T-Mobile," she says. Before those conversations, Callie says, she was blind to those experiences. "That's part of my privilege," she says. "I don't have to worry about that experience of low-level abuse. I have felt just how polarizing our country is and the impact that that has on the confidence and well-being of my employees."

After hearing about employees' experiences, Callie didn't spring to immediate action. Instead, she realized that the appropriate next step was to sit with what she had heard to truly acknowledge and process it. She also pushed back against her natural, but ultimately unhelpful, reaction: shame. "I think there's a natural tendency to feel shame. But in feeling that shame, we want to brush it off or excuse it or get to fixing it." When leaders spring to action or put Band-Aids on the problem, they don't do the work of fully understanding the problem. She had to keep listening.

"Part of the problem is that corporations don't talk about racism and don't listen to employees. They don't have a way to identify what policies might have racist effects. There was a lot of truth-telling that had to occur with us being accountable for the whiteness of our team and also we had to engage with our employees on what we were going to do about that.

"It's hard work," she says. "We're not there yet, but it has been an extremely important conversation and an important investment in personal development and learning for me."

Courageous listening

If you're asking people to speak freely about hard topics, you really need courage on two sides. Clearly, you need the courage of the person who is speaking up. But you also need the audience to be courageous *listeners*.

Being a courageous listener means opening yourself to hearing what the other person has to say, full stop—listening even if you don't agree or don't want to hear the bad news they're delivering or if what they're saying makes you feel ashamed or guilty or uncomfortable, sitting and seeping in what they're sharing without immediately reacting with *your* feelings or jumping up to propose solutions. Hear them first. Courageous listening is the first step toward atonement and reconciliation.

As Stephen Tang, former CEO of OraSure, says, it's "being in the market for the unvarnished truth." That takes courage.

MAKE ROOM FOR DIFFICULT CONVERSATIONS

Crystal Ashby advocates for courageous, uncomfortable conversations—between outsiders and insiders, minority and majority groups, dominant and nondominant cultures.

Here's what she has seen at organizations where these hard conversations are encouraged: "People are sharing exactly how they feel. They know that they're being heard." In other words, they feel *belonging*. "Belonging is about finding their real space in an organization. It's the ability to be authentic, to be themselves, to bring their whole selves to work."

I see belonging as the currency of impact for the individual. We may have big-picture conversations as a firm, a country, and a world about social justice. But for the individual person, nothing changes at work unless they feel a sense of improved belonging in their day-to-day relationships.

How can leaders know if they're succeeding in having these honest, difficult conversations and creating a new sense of belonging?

"If you aren't hearing something that gives you a moment for pause, you haven't asked all the right questions," Crystal says. "No entity is devoid of [racial inequality]. It is a part of the fabric of who we are."

→**TRY THIS:** Even though the summer of reckoning of 2020 is over, it continues to be crucial to facilitate difficult conversations about racial injustice at work. Use the guidelines below to plan regular conversations with your teams. Remember, the goal is belonging, and no one will feel like they belong if they don't feel heard.

- ◆ **Start with reflection.** If you're talking about a heated or difficult topic, ask everyone to do some personal reflection before the conversation. Get people started by offering a few reflection questions. For example:

  Consider the following statements, and select the one that best describes how you feel:
  - I would rather not talk about difference: race/racism, gender, sexual orientation/identity, ability, and so on.
  - I am very uncomfortable talking about race/racism, gender, sexual orientation/identity, ability, and so on.
  - I am usually uncomfortable talking about race/racism, gender, sexual orientation/identity, ability, and so on.
  - I am sometimes uncomfortable talking about race/racism, gender, sexual orientation/identity, ability, and so on.
  - I am usually comfortable talking about race/racism, gender, sexual orientation/identity, ability, and so on.

- I am very comfortable talking about race/racism, gender, sexual orientation/identity, ability, and so on.

  Try finishing these sentences:
- The hard part of talking about race/racism, gender, sexual orientation/identity, ability, and so on is

  _____

- The beneficial part of talking about race/racism, gender, sexual orientation/identity, ability, and so on is

  _____

  After reflecting on your own comfort level, think about how you will stay engaged when the topic of race/ racism, gender, sexual orientation/identity, ability, and so on arises:
- Do you feel ill-prepared to talk about race/racism, gender, sexual orientation/identity, ability, and so on?
- If so, commit to learning more about the issues by reading, studying history, following current events, and brushing up on equality and inclusion work.
- Do you reroute discussions when you sense discomfort in the room? If so, commit to riding out the discussion next time.

◆ **Agree to the Chatham House Rule.** Agree as a group that you can use the information shared in your discussions but that you won't identify or affiliate any participant with specific comments they made.

◆ **Get on the same page about your guiding principles.** If you're leading the conversation, share the purpose behind the discussion (for example, to allow a forum to continue the conversations around allyship and dig deeper into important topics).

◆ **Model vulnerability.** If you feel comfortable, share a personal story that supports the broader themes.

Your DE&I dictionary

◆ *Diversity* is a statistic.
◆ *Inclusion* is a verb. It's where the real work happens. Inclusion is a set of intentions, actions, and programs.
◆ And then, you reach *belonging*. Belonging is the real promised land.

ALIGN YOUR ACTIONS WITH YOUR PURPOSE

After acknowledging the injustice in your own organization and listening to diverse experiences and perspectives, it's time to make a plan and take action. At T-Mobile, Callie Field says leaders have been working to figure out where systems and processes exist that have the effect of being racist.

She says the company's leaders are asking, "How are we going to hold ourselves accountable for being a more equitable place and for allowing people who have experienced racism or who are underrepresented to have access and opportunity?"

Brian Tippens sees a new sophistication in how leaders think about weaving social values into the organization's work. In other words, lip service won't cut it. "It can't just be about how we're going to create some pipeline programs to hire for diversity or how we're going to have some employee resource groups to celebrate cultural celebrations throughout the year. It has to be really viewing diversity and inclusion as a business imperative at all levels."

Leaders should ask themselves specific questions, including the following:

◆ What is the change we're committing to?
◆ What do we want to be different?
◆ How will we make this change a business imperative like every other business imperative?

- How will we turn this from a nice idea into something that actually happens? How will we measure progress?
- How will I, as an individual leader, commit to making a change? How will I own my part in this action?

MEASURE WHAT MATTERS

If you're talking about making big changes to your culture, Crystal Ashby says it's important to measure your progress and tie your success to compensation, just like any other performance metric. If diversity, inclusion, and equity are going to be priorities, you have to measure and reward them. Otherwise, employees will see your initiatives and goals as just hollow talk.

One mistake that Crystal warns against: celebrating false wins. In the past, she says, "diversity" has been a goal, but only certain groups have really made strides. In particular, white women have moved into leadership roles—but they haven't brought others along. "If you disaggregate the data, one of the things you're going to find is that the gender piece will actually skew the numbers greatly. You have to break it out by Black, Brown, Latinx, LGBTQ, Asian, Native American. You have to look at those individually because that gives you the true story about how you're doing. And I suspect when you do that, not everybody is doing as well as they thought because, let's be honest, if you talk about diversity and inclusion, white women have been the beneficiaries of it for years. They are the number one beneficiary of the diversity and inclusion environment."

As you make a plan to become a more equitable organization, you'll hit bumps on the road. No organization is going to erase decades of injustice overnight. Focus on progress, not perfection. "This is not about companies being perfect," says Kathryn Minshew, co-founder of The Muse. "It's not necessarily about being a 10 out of 10 on every dimension tomorrow, but it is about organizations having a clear sense of what they want to become and that they're communicating that to their team, being transparent and being honest."

We should all acknowledge that diversity and inclusion, justice, and joy aren't goals that will be met overnight. There's a lot of change that needs to happen, and sometimes change is slow. "This is a real journey we're going to have to commit to being on, and we're going to have to continue to come back and have the conversation," Crystal Ashby says. "We're going to have to admit when we're wrong. We're going to have to admit when mistakes were made. We're going to have to ask how we change it and fix it. But we're all going to do it together."

Hope for the future

Crystal lays out the truth, but she's not judging anyone. Instead, she wants to help change the narrative. If we really want to build stronger, more just, more joyful organizations, we have to face the difficult truth and change the conversation. "The conversation has to be started by people who have the power right now," she says.

Her hope? That we forget about returning to "normal" after the tumult of the pandemic. The pandemic forced a pause—to rethink and reevaluate. "We should not come out the same as we went into this. We should learn the lessons. We should have spent the time really digging deep and saying, 'How do we make this place a better place for everyone?'"

She hopes for a commitment to real growth, change, and justice. To more joy. "We need to make sure we come out of this crisis stronger, wiser, more in touch with humanity, more in touch with each other, more connected to each other."

Brian Tippens says he feels hopeful about the future of hard conversations at work. "I think there's optimism simply in the fact that we're having conversations [about diversity, inclusion, and social justice] in a way that we weren't a couple of years ago," he says. "Dealing with adversity is causing us as corporations, and as individuals, to think about how we can be a force for good."

Kathryn Minshew hopes that leaders take this opportunity to ignite real change. "We cannot build companies that best represent and serve the diversity of the world if we don't turn that same focus towards building the diversity of our teams. This is a precious and painfully won opportunity for us all to be better, and I really hope that we take it."

As the late civil rights leader and congressman John Lewis wrote, "Ours is not the struggle of one day, one week, or one year. Ours is not the struggle of one judicial appointment or presidential term. Ours is the struggle of a lifetime, or maybe even many lifetimes, and each one of us in every generation must do our part."

Globally, we're all part of a human movement to achieve our highest aspirations. Part of that journey is acknowledging our blind spots. By recognizing injustices and standing up as allies for each other, we can create reckoning, reconciliation, hope, and positive change.

Find some joy in every day. *At the end of the day, if you haven't found the joy, pause because you missed it. Don't miss it when it happens.*
                            —Crystal Ashby, former CEO of the Executive
                                          Leadership Council (ELC)

SECTION THREE

What's Next for Joy at Work?

In this book so far, we have covered what the research tells us about joy at work; how we can drive joy at work; and the state of joy at work in a complex world, changed forever by a global pandemic. Now let's look to the future. We know the path that has led us here. What comes next? How could we create a real shift toward joy? We'll look at innovation at work, which I see as the ultimate driver of joy, and we'll look ahead to the next generation, to whom the baton is being passed now. How will they make their mark on the workplace as we know it and create a meaningful shift toward joy?

CHAPTER 10

The Joy of Innovation

The nature of business now is change—constant, continuous, transformative change. We could look at change as scary, unwelcome, or threatening. But I try to think about change as a natural way to keep ourselves alive. Adapting is the only option. And it's invigorating in all key ways.

If we want to build innovative companies that outpace the competition, stay ahead of the curve, and radically rethink traditional industries, we need people on our teams who are inspired, excited, and motivated to think differently.

Joy is the unlock for radical innovation.

Let's look at a few examples of leaders and organizations that are going all in on drastic innovation and powering it with a joy mindset.

Leapfrog your legacy

You might be thinking that innovation is just for people who work at start-ups or in tech. Not so.

My go-to source for all things innovation at my firm is Michael Roemer. Michael leads Kearney's innovation hub,

FFWD. He has found inspiration from companies with long histories that are able to shift so dramatically from their past that they "leapfrog their legacy," completely reinventing themselves and moving from slow traditionalists to upstart innovators.

Daimler AG, the company that makes Mercedes Benz, is an example of a company that is leapfrogging its legacy. The company started way back in 1926. Nearly 100 years later, in 2019, when Ola Källenius took on the role of CEO, he made a bold move. Instead of running a company that sold many kinds of vehicles (including trucks, buses, and low-cost cars), he announced a major pivot: Daimler would only focus on luxury cars. The strategy was simple: create a narrow focus, get it right, and win.

He made big changes to the company's leadership structure, reducing the number of leaders and flattening the hierarchy through a shorter reporting structure. Through that focus, he was able to create a different environment for innovation, mobilize the company toward a drastically new future, and leapfrog the old company legacy.

Look for new ideas in unexpected places

When I asked Michael about how to build a culture of innovation, he stressed the importance of finding new ideas in unexpected places.

One way that leaders can keep themselves primed to find new ideas? By spending time *not* working. Michael pointed me to a Harvard Business School study that clocked how CEOs spent their time.[1] The study's authors underscore the importance of downtime—for thinking, reflecting, and ruminating.

---

[1]Michael E. Porter and Nitin Nohria, "How CEOs Manage Time," *Harvard Business Review*, July–August 2018, https://hbr.org/2018/07/how-ceos-manage-time

We paid special attention to the 25 percent of time—or roughly six hours a day—when CEOs were awake and not working. Typically, they spent about half those hours with their families, and most had learned to become very disciplined about this. Most also found at least some hours (2.1 a day, on average) for downtime, which included everything from watching television and reading for pleasure, to hobbies like photography.

The CEO's job is mentally and physically demanding. Activities that preserve elements of normal life keep CEOs grounded and better able to engage with colleagues and workers—as opposed to distant, detached, and disconnected. CEOs also have to make time for their own professional renewal and development (which our data showed was often the biggest casualty of a packed schedule).

It takes a lot of discipline to make regular time away from work to spur your creative juices. But in order to be innovative (and, I'd argue, to be truly joyful), time away is essential. We have to remember that a good idea can come from anywhere—an article you read, a trip you take, a conversation you overhear. But we have to give ourselves the space to recognize those ideas. That's why even when my own work and travel schedule is busy, I am relentless about carving out time for a run outside every day and a short bike ride around the neighborhood in between scheduled meetings. It's when I do my best thinking, frankly. Lately, I've added daily rejuvenation time in the sauna when I'm able and infrared is at full strength. I come out of the sauna with a new energy, ready to take on the next portion of my day and think more creatively.

Research from the past few decades supports the idea that people need time, space, and freedom in order to innovate.

Kearney's "Best Innovator" research from 2011 identified "space for innovation" as a key element of an innovation culture. Employees need freedom to innovate.[2]

My vision of an innovative future includes calm, creative thinking time in every person's daily routine. Leaders should set that example by making space in their own schedules for downtime. We cannot expect people to be joyfully creative at work without creating the time and space for innovation. Give yourself and the people around you the space to find ideas in unexpected places.

Stay at the edge

I have learned that pushing people to innovate is a delicate art. You can't put someone in a big role or give them a challenge when they're completely out of their depth. But there's also danger in staying in our comfort zones for too long. It's a balance.

Behavioral scientist Jon Levy gives this advice: "The key is to be just at the edge of your capability so that you're constantly learning and growing."

At the edge. I like that image. If we want to build companies that are at the cutting edge, we have to challenge ourselves to be at our own leading edge, leaning into new ideas, growth, and learning.

Here's the metaphor Jon shared, which he credits to Shane Snow, author of *Smartcuts: How Hackers, Innovators, and Icons Accelerate Success*: "On a jungle gym, you want the bars far enough apart that you can swing and catch them. But not so far that you'll fall off the jungle gym and not so close that

---

[2]Kearney, Innovation: A solid wager, in good times and in bad, https://www.kearney.com/operations-performance-transformation/article?/a/innovation-a-solid-wager-in-good-times-and-in-bad

you can't build momentum. It's in the momentum," Jon says. "If I suddenly put you on a jungle gym in the middle, you might not be able to reach the next bar because you don't have any momentum. It's the same way with careers. If I suddenly put somebody who's completely unqualified as a senior vice president, they'll have no momentum and experience to keep them going. They'll fail."

That's my call to every leader who wants to build both joy *and* innovation. Think about how you'll help your teams make it across the monkey bars.

Empower people to innovate

We talked in Chapter 3 about autonomous work, and the high likelihood that people will feel joy at work if they have control and autonomy. Stephen Tang, former CEO of OraSure, sees autonomy as a baseline requirement for innovative teams.

He says that the two tenets of autonomous, innovative teams are accountability and empowerment. "In other words, you're accountable for what we jointly agree are your objectives, and you're empowered to make them happen," he says. That combination of clear accountability and empowerment results in what Stephen calls a "high-velocity decision-making environment" where people can work across the organization to find the answers they need, adapt during times of crisis, and build trust quickly.

Look at purpose through the lens of innovation

Finally, I think purpose and innovation are inextricably linked. Earlier, in Chapter 5, we talked about the motivating power of purpose. If you have a big purpose and a big objective—a big WHY and a goal you want to meet—you're going to need big, bold, innovative action to get there.

Every innovator I know has something pushing them forward. They stand *for* something. Their work is powered by purpose and fueled by innovation.

> *There are ups and downs in business. The job of the leader is to modulate those a bit, to be a steady hand. But I can't deny that I feel both the ups and the downs strongly. I cope by doing what I was taught growing up:* **count your blessings.** *I'm a great believer that if you send gratitude out there, it comes back to you manyfold. That's what keeps me juiced and keeps me moving.*
>
> —Stephen Tang, former CEO of OraSure

CHAPTER 11

The Next Generation of Joy at Work

How will the next generation change the way we think about work, and how will they infuse work with more joy, justice, equality, and positive change?

Pass the baton

I'm extremely focused on the next generation that will soon lead Kearney, the firm I've been a part of for the past 25 years. Here's why: Kearney is a private partnership—with an emphasis on *partner*. Our goal is to build a firm that will outlast us by multiple generations. For that reason, I am extremely motivated to build a firm that is ready for the long haul and to coach and guide the next generation of colleagues who will lead it. I think of my work as a relay race to the next generation. I want this institution to outlast me and take on a purpose that is bigger than myself.

When I think about my legacy as a leader, I want to attract the best people to carry on the firm's mission. Years from now, when people hear my name, I want them to have a smile on their face.

This chapter is for the leaders who are in my shoes, preparing to hand over the baton. But it's also for the next generation: the members of Gen X, Gen Y, and Gen Z who are taking the reins, demanding a better way of working, and who are already making a serious impact on the world.

Join the "Great Resignation"—or is it the "Great Reflection"?

We can't talk about the youngest generations in the workforce without talking about the much-publicized "Great Resignation" of 2021 and 2022 (and beyond?). You likely have experienced the Great Resignation firsthand. This trend of employees leaving for greener pastures has certainly affected Kearney, too. But I don't think of it as a Great Resignation. I think of it as a Great Reflection.

Millions of people realized they had a unique opportunity to consider their *ikigai*: what they're good at versus what the world needs; what they can get paid for versus what they're passionate about.

When people were running from meeting to meeting all day, they didn't have time to step back and notice that they were climbing the wrong ladder all along. The pandemic showed many people that the ladder was against the wrong wall.

This trend is impacting every sector. An IMF report from early 2022 predicts, "Workers who dropped out of in-person service professions (for example, leisure and hospitality) during the pandemic may be unwilling to return, leading to potential labor shortages in those industries."[1] People are not going to put up with being overworked and underpaid. They're not settling for the "anything less than joy" that we've discussed in this book.

---

[1] International Monetary Fund, "Rising Caseloads, a Disrupted Recovery, and Higher Inflation," January 2022, https://www.imf.org/en/Publications/WEO/Issues/2022/01/25/world-economic-outlook-update-january-2022

Dr. Anthony Wilbon, dean of Howard School of Business, sees students and young alumni rethinking their definition of success to include much more flexibility at work. "People are migrating toward companies that are recreating work-life balance," he says. "They're attracted to organizations that are creating environments with more flexibility. The younger generations are willing to take the leap and move around to find what they want."

And he has realized that even his business students might not want to pursue business roles. "Over the last few years, I've determined that not everybody is interested in climbing the ladder to the corporate space. We have students who are interested in entrepreneurship. I have students who are interested in nonprofit management. We've been training students to get into corporate spaces ever since our existence, 50 years now. That's what we do very well. But now we're trying to provide a little bit of flexibility" by helping students identify different opportunities, he says.

As I listen to the next generation, I realize that the Great Resignation isn't the problem. It's a symptom. As leaders, we have to address the root problems. People are reflecting that they're not getting what they need from work. I think that's why the concept of *ikigai* resonated with a lot of the people in our firm. It's a concept that has been around for hundreds of years. But these are the questions we should be asking ourselves all the time.

Kathryn Minshew, a Millennial and co-founder of The Muse, had her own Great Reflection early in the pandemic. She realized she needed to reconnect with her core purpose. "I think you've got to remind yourself what matters," she says. "What is the core, the essence of what I do? What am I trying to change or make better in the world? And that big picture has really driven me. I just keep trying to ground myself and take small measurable steps."

And she sees this Great Reflection happening broadly: "People are not just opting out of work. They're reaffirming what they care about, and then making changes that are in alignment with their priorities and values."

One of those values: a personalized experience of work. Kathryn says that given our current culture, it's not surprising that the next generation expects a more personalized work experience. Our tech products, such as Netflix, are acutely personalized to our history and tastes. "We're used to a world where a lot of the products we use and experiences we have are trying to understand what we want and give it to us."

So when young people encounter a one-size-fits-all workplace, with one identical experience for everyone, they want something different. In other words, she says, there is no one "workforce." The workforce is made up of unique individuals; we may be able to group them into general cohorts, but all employees are not the same. "There's a cohort of the workforce that prioritizes flexibility above anything else. There's also a cohort that's prioritizing learning and growth opportunities. And there *are* people who are still prioritizing compensation."

Kathryn says this vision of a diverse workforce looking for a wide range of priorities is actually a hopeful message for employers, especially smaller companies. "You can compete really effectively by figuring out what you want to compete on, and being really good at that one thing. You don't have to be a 10 out of 10 on every metric that job seekers are seeking."

In other words, as we all reflect on what we really want from our work, and what impact we want to make on the world—our own *ikigai* equation—answers will be different for everyone. Gen Y and Gen Z don't want one copy-paste experience. The key is finding the people who want the specific purpose, mission, style, and experience that you offer and who bring the matching set of skills, preferences, and ideas that your organization needs.

→ **TRY THIS:** If you're feeling jaded about hiring and retaining the next generation or if you're not sure what new employees are looking for, stop trying to be everything to everyone. Help your organization get crystal clear on its core purpose and strengths.

What are you trying to accomplish, who do you need to help you get there, and what can you offer them?

Promote that specific mission and specific incentives, and you'll likely find the people who are the right match.

Shift the balance of power

The old dynamic between employee and employer is shifting below our feet. The power dynamic and the social contract between employee and employer are evolving.

Kathryn Minshew and the team at The Muse are keeping a close eye on the changing relationship between employees and employers: "A shorthand we use is 'relationships over transactions.' Broadly, it means that the old model (labor in exchange for a paycheck) is no longer serving most people. And instead, individuals are looking for their employers to provide much more. They're looking for learning and growth, flexibility, a broader sense of meaning, and much more human workplaces. People are looking for employers who share their values."

When I talked with Kathryn in 2020, during the height of the pandemic lockdowns in the United States, she told me that employees were building "whisper networks" to share information about how companies were *actually* treating their employees, no matter what their published statements about their values might say. I saw a similar trend happening—a "Yelpification" of work culture, where people will tell leaders exactly what they see that's broken or unappealing about working at the organization. These observations showed me, clear and simple: there was a shift in power. And the talent has the power now.

The next generation is also lobbying for major changes in who holds the power inside organizations. They're not accepting the homogenous leadership that hasn't changed in decades. And I agree with them. I see it this way: power is about who's in the room. The dominant culture has the power. The next generation has pointed out this fact, and they're ready to change it. They're pointing out that if we want to build an inclusive society, we need to change who has a seat at the table. That makes a lot of sense to me.

Keep your promises

Another shift? Employees expect and demand authenticity from the organizations where they work. And if their expectations pre-hire aren't matched when they start working, they will not stick around.

The Muse released research in 2022 that reveals a wave of "shift shock," the experience when someone starts a new job, and it is nothing like what they expected.[2] Seventy-two percent of people said they had experienced shift shock. And 80 percent said it's acceptable to leave a new job before six months if it doesn't live up to your expectations.

"Candidates are getting more comfortable voting with their feet if they're unhappy with an employer. And they have more power to spread the word," Kathryn says.

---

[2]Devin Tomb, "72% of Muse Survey Respondents Say They've Experienced 'Shift Shock,'" The Muse, https://www.themuse.com/advice/shift-shock-muse-survey-2022

Put your values into action

In Chapter 5, we discussed the power of purpose. The younger generations are looking for organizations with a clear purpose and values—and the actions to back them up.

"Gen Z is very values-aligned," Kathryn Minshew says. "When they search for a job, they want to find a company that offers paid maternity leave, or tuition reimbursement, or that are female-founded or veteran-founded or Black-founded. A lot of job candidates, especially Millennial and Gen Z candidates, are also asking how the company is doing on measures of racial justice and diversity and inclusion."

If your organization doesn't have good answers to those questions, it's time to get to work. Because, as Kathryn points out, "these questions aren't going away. The trend is not changing. Younger talent is becoming bolder in asking companies to respond to social issues, asking how companies are doing."

Make culture a nonnegotiable

Much of this book has been about the broader idea of "culture." But it's important to note that younger generations are demanding work cultures that are aspirational and that reward the best human behavior.

To avoid toxic cultures and build something better, we cannot tolerate bad behavior. Culture can't be the lowest common denominator of behaviors we tolerate. It should be a bridge that leads to purpose, meaning, and belonging.

How can organizations prioritize culture? One way is to put culture-focused, people-focused leadership into the most executive roles. Kathryn Parsons, founder of Decoded, shared this example with me: Leena Nair, who was chief human resources officer at Unilever and embodied the company's values, was hired by Chanel as CEO. "I think this is the beginning of a trend," Kathryn says. We're going to see those individuals who put culture and joy and lifelong learning at the center of their business strategies increasingly being brought in to lead the entire organization, not just the HR function."

Why? Because "retaining and attracting the best talent in the world is going to become a business-critical issue," she says. Keeping talent is going to be about "their values, their purpose, and how much they enjoy the day-to-day of how they're working."

Building a strong, sustainable culture is a necessary foundation for anything else you want to do with your organization because if the culture isn't right, people won't stick around.

Rethink old trade-offs

As Kathryn Minshew mentioned, the old trade-offs of labor for a paycheck are changing. Dr. Ashley Whillans knows a lot about the trade-offs that young people are willing—and aren't willing—to make at work. The Harvard Business School professor and author of *Time Smart* researches how the daily and long-term decisions that people make about time and money in their personal lives, relationships, and at work impact their well-being. She says we're at an inflection point.

"My students are enthralled and enraptured with these ideas around flexibility, remote work, happiness, and seeking purpose through our work. These trends have accelerated during the pandemic. Students who were impacted directly and indirectly by the pandemic are more passionate than ever about seeking work not just for financial security, but also for purpose in life." Her advice is simple: "Prioritize free time and happiness just as you would prioritize work. We need to feel as comfortable negotiating for time as we do for money."

"It is important to take time each day to make sure we're living our life in a way that's aligned with our broader goals and purpose," she says. "Cultivating time and social relationships are key ways to improve happiness. I don't necessarily see work and time in opposition with one another. If we do really want ambitious careers and also a strong personal life, we have to put equal weight and equal effort into both our professional pursuits and our personal pursuits."

What about blowback from managers and colleagues? Will taking more time off make you look like a less-dedicated team member? Ashley says that the data shows the opposite: "As long as we're asking for more time proactively, our colleagues see us as more committed because at the end of the day, quality really is the key metric."

And, she says, you can't defer joy. It doesn't work to tell yourself "I'll work now, and I'll have fun/spend time with my family/contribute to my community *later*."

"I so often hear my students say, 'All of this prioritization of family and social interactions and time sounds nice, but I need to pay off my student loan. I want to get to a certain salary band, and then I'll start prioritizing time, then I'll start doing the things that really matter.' The problem is, when you get to that salary band, your reference point is going to change. Your lifestyle will have already changed, your spending habits will have already changed, so you're going to need even more money. This if–then thinking is a bit of a time trap because our reference points, our goals, are always going to be fundamentally shifting. If we do that if–then thinking, we'll probably never actually follow through on those passions that we've always wanted to [pursue]."

So, she says, the only answer is to make time for what matters to you *today*. Right now. Spend 30 minutes every day cultivating your interests, spending time with people you care about, or whatever else matters most to you. If 30 minutes isn't realistic, could you try 10 minutes a day?

If you can do that, Ashley says you'll likely find more joy every day. "Breaking down big, broad goals into small, actionable steps and then substituting some of the ways we waste time on an everyday basis, like social media, and inserting that time with all of these other goals can be a really helpful strategy to make sure we're walking the talk now in our lives."

Her research shows this trend, but she also learned it through personal experience. "I myself did this," she says. "For the first several years in my career, I did not set boundaries. I put all of my attention and energy and effort into work. I was basically attached to my work. I would go to my inbox instead of spending time with my partner over dinner or going for a walk. Those small decisions really add up over time, both positively and negatively." She realized she needed to make a change for the sake of her happiness and the health of her relationships. Now, she says, "I make concerted efforts to disconnect at certain times of day, to clearly communicate my boundaries to my colleagues, and also to clearly communicate my off time to my partner so we can coordinate on our schedules. The future is uncertain, but the present moment is something we all have available to us."

→**TRY THIS:** Want more joy in your life? The research shows that spending even a few additional minutes a day on your most important priorities will boost joy. Try spending 10 minutes a day on the parts of your life that matter most to you. Trade those 10 p.m. work emails for reading the book that's been on your list for months. Spend the hour after dinner with your spouse, friends, or kids—no working allowed. Build in habits that prioritize your personal relationships and interests, and stick to them.

Accept change as a constant

Finally, I'll address anyone who is still feeling a little grumpy about the way change is racing through our work. My advice: Accept that change is our new constant. Accept that we all want different things. I have had to learn and accept that the newer generations (in my firm and elsewhere) might want very different things than what I wanted. They want a different life, and they feel comfortable asking for it. They're more willing to say it out loud. My generation was taught to go with the flow, but now we're getting recruits who want to talk about purpose and values. I think that's fabulous, and it's an opportunity for the best organizations to respond quickly and move forward with the most promising talent.

> *We have to be able to **lower our guards, reach out to the people around us**, and share joys and pains so that we can all work together towards a common goal.*
>
> —Anthony Wilbon, dean of the
> Howard School of Business

Conclusion

When I took on the job of managing partner and chairman at Kearney back in 2018, my message to my colleagues was simple: Take pure joy in your work.

The *Financial Times* wrote an article about my new tenure and included this challenge: "Joy is an unusual word to hear from a corporate leader."

I say that it was a challenge because I've always known that we shouldn't settle for anything less than joy at work. I try to be joyfully relentless about whatever matters to me. Whatever I do, I'm going to give it my best and wholehearted passion. After all, I've chosen my path. It's up to me to find and create joy along the way. Without joy, what else really matters?

And I work in an industry that I think is inherently joyful. Consulting is all about helping companies and societies create their success stories. How heady is that? And I get to work with talented and dedicated colleagues who I know won't let me down. That's work to be grateful for.

As I think about what I want to be remembered for—my "echoes in eternity," to quote from the movie *Gladiator*— I think about making things better. My parents believed that every generation should make life better for their children. That's a focus of mine, too. I try to live that legacy. For the people at my firm, I want to create an atmosphere where people can be confident and bold, full of purpose. I want to be a multiplier of joy.

For the next generation more broadly, my hope is that you can determine your own source of joy. Find a job you want, pick a workplace that makes sense for *you*, be yourself, and run your own race. Define your own success and joy. Don't waste your time following anyone else's obligation or path.

We're living in a culture of comparison, which can be incredibly damaging to our psyches. Studies about social media show us that constant envy and comparison lead to despair, not to joy. When we're focused on what other people have, we don't have time to realize who we are, what we care about, and what we can do to create our own happiness now.

You have to be your own board of directors. You have to be the person who determines your own destiny. You have to be true to yourself. There are a million books and movies written about that aphorism because it's true. You know who you are better than anyone else. So don't compare yourself to anyone else. Don't outsource your happiness.

And if you're responsible for other people, lift them up and help them find their path to joy. Your obligation is to create the circumstances for joy: to make it possible for *others* to run their own race, find belonging, and be themselves. People fundamentally want to be fulfilled. As a leader, you can be a multiplier of joy.

My final advice for you: I have learned that gratitude is the wellspring of joy. Make a list of all the things you're grateful for. Then try to live in the moment and be grateful for that moment. If you're always trying to chase the next rainbow, you'll miss the joy in your life right now.

Be hungry. Be humble. And always run your own race.

About the Author

Alex Liu is managing partner and chairman at Kearney, a leading global consulting partnership.

A trusted advisor to CEOs and boards for over 30 years, Alex is the firm's ninth managing partner in its nearly 100-year history, first elected in 2018. An immigrant from Taiwan who was raised in the South, he also serves as the firm's chief diversity officer. His long career in tech and telecoms has allowed him to work in over 70 countries, including service on public and private boards.

Recognized by *Consulting* magazine as a global Top 25 Consultant and by the Global Diversity List as one of the top 10 senior executives, he is also a top-ranked consulting CEO. A regular contributor to the World Economic Forum, he has been featured in the *Harvard Business Review, Financial Times*, the *Economist*, CNBC, and Bloomberg. He regularly consults with business and public sector leaders on matters of leadership, culture, justice, and joy, and hosts an award-winning podcast, Joy@Work.

Hailing from generations of educators and coaches, he boasts three adult children in San Diego who carry on that same family legacy in different ways. Alex earned a BA in economics from Yale and an MBA from Harvard, after graduating from Episcopal High School in Virginia. He remains an avid rugby player and Tar Heels basketball fan.

Index

Page number followed by f indicate figure